ABOUT THE AUTHORS

Doris Pozzi has over ten years' professional experience as a consultant. She has extensive experience in organizational and market research, marketing, communications strategy, and personal and organizational change. She has worked as a workshop facilitator and designed and run training programs in personal growth and organizational change.

Doris holds a Bachelor of Science with honors in Psychology and a Masters in Educational Psychology, both from The University of Melbourne. She has been a registered psychologist for eight years.

Doris is managing director of a management consulting company providing psychological products and consulting services for personal and organizational development. She is a trustee of the Community Aid Abroad Ethical Investment Trust, and volunteers her time to supervise trainee psychologists.

Stephen Williams has a background in engineering, management and marketing and has worked in a range of company settings. He has developed and conducted training workshops for many professionals, with courses including training in the application of information technology and in management systems to improve workplace efficiency. For the past ten years, he has worked in consulting. Stephen has a Bachelor of Engineering with honors from The University of Melbourne.

Combined with his other experience, Stephen has over ten years' experience in radio and is a collector of '60s rhythm and blues recordings.

Doris and Stephen are married. They have lived and worked together in India on rural development projects and have also been active in community development and fund-raising. Their company is a corporate sponsor of *The Big Issue*, a bi-weekly magazine sold by homeless and ex-homeless people, and a corporate member of The Epoch Foundation, an organization promoting ethical practices and spirituality in business.

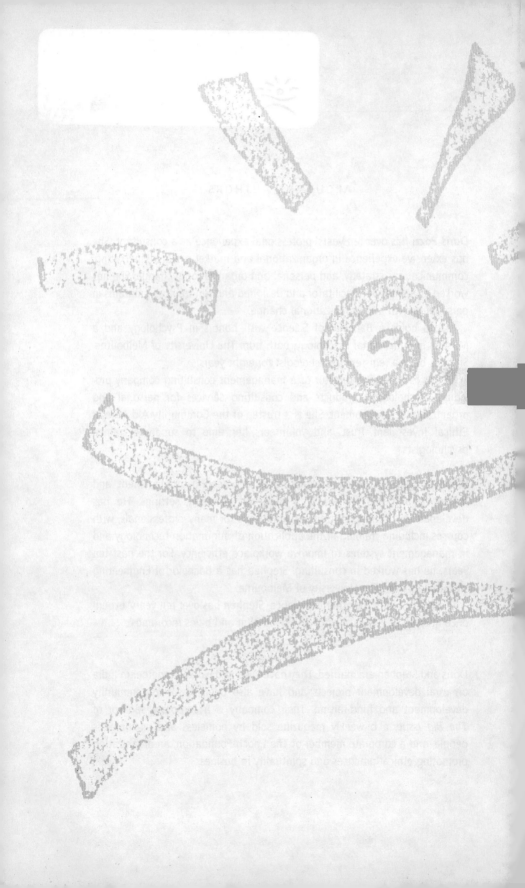

SUCCESS WITH SOUL

NEW INSIGHTS TO ACHIEVING SUCCESS WITH REAL MEANING

Doris Pozzi and Stephen Williams

Dorian Welles Pty Ltd

MELBOURNE   SEATTLE

Published by Dorian Welles Pty Ltd
652 Drummond Street, Carlton North, Melbourne 3054, Australia
E-mail: soulman@werple.net.au
2313B 10th Ave East, Seattle, WA 98102, USA
E-mail: burbidge@aol.com

First published 1997
Produced in Hong Kong by Sino Publishing House
Project management: The Greenglades Group
Edited by Cathy Smith
Cover design by Marcus Lee Design and R.T.J. Klinkhamer
Text design by R.T.J. Klinkhamer
Typeset by Emtype Desktop Publishing Services

Library of Congress cataloguing in publication data

Pozzi, Doris.
Success with soul: new insights to achieving success
with real meaning/Doris Pozzi and Stephen Williams.
  p. cm.
Includes bibliographical references.
ISBN 0-646-28692-7
1. Success–Psychological aspects. 2. Success–Religious aspects.
3. Self-actualization (Psychology). I. Williams, Stephen.
II. Title.
BF637.S8 1997   97-60118
158.1   CIP

National Library of Australia Cataloguing-in-Publication data

Pozzi, Doris, 1962– .
  Success with soul: new insights to achieving personal
  success with real meaning.

  Bibliography.
  ISBN 0 646 28692 7.

  1. Self-actualization (Psychology). 2. Success. 3. Success –
  Religious aspects. I. Williams, Stephen, 1961– .
  II. Dorian Welles (Firm). III. Title.

158.1

The Soul. The principle of life in humans or animals.

Shorter Oxford Dictionary

Soul. That dimension of ourselves concerned with meaning.

Doris Pozzi and Stephen Williams

Contents

Preface

Welcome to *Success With Soul*.

Those of us interested in personal growth recognize it as a journey. It's a bit like world exploration – searching for the source of the Amazon, hacking through the jungles of Borneo, crossing the deserts of Africa. Both the inner journey and the outer journey are about exploring uncharted territory, where we incorporate new learning and insights and grow as individuals. We are also keen to explore the new challenges that affect our lives; challenges such as those created by technology and social change.

One thing is certain: successful explorers are well equipped, both physically and mentally. *Success With Soul* is designed to equip you for the explorer's life. It does not tell you where to explore – that's up to you – but it will help you make your plan, assemble the necessary equipment and enjoy the journey along the way. It will help you think about success and soul in a new way, a way that will help you to move forward. This new way is not about turning your back on success in the pursuit of soul. It is about weaving a rich tapestry where soul and success are integrally entwined.

Recent research has provided new insights and practical solutions that enable you to resolve personal contradictions that are holding you back, contradictions as fundamental as the one between success and soul. In *Success With Soul* we provide a detailed analysis of the underlying dynamics that can make you feel trapped and which are intimately related to personal direction, alignment and meaning. Along the way we will also show why strategies such as attempting to live a balanced lifestyle are not the answer to achieving personal success with real meaning.

The focus of *Success With Soul* is on providing long-term benefits, not just "quick fixes", and we do not present theory without also presenting solutions and methods that people can implement in their own lives. More than ten years of involvement in this field has convinced us that – along with theory – people want principles and methods that work.

Success With Soul is, in many ways, a synthesis of our professional and personal experiences. The ideas and activities presented here have been tested and refined over many years. Many have been used successfully by individuals in a range of family, community and organizational settings and by people in all age groups. As authors, we feel our responsibility is to provide people with proven techniques for personal growth. We personally use all of the activities presented in this book in our own lives. They shape our lives as well as the lives of others.

Furthermore, *Success With Soul* is not about trying to become more "soulful" in an abstract kind of way; nor is it about trying to relax through meditation; or about just "smelling the roses" along the way. While these "soul activities" can certainly contribute to life's richness, they don't address the foundations – it's like giving an old house a new coat of paint when the roof has holes in it and the walls are falling in.

Creating real success with soul in our lives requires planning, action and personal reflection: in essence, re-weaving the fabric of our lives through different ways of knowing, doing and being. This re-weaving leads to more enduring, fulfilling relationships, meaningful endeavors and happiness.

We believe *Success With Soul* will help you develop a deeper understanding of what success and soul mean to you. Along with a number of important insights, we have included tools for determining your personal values and your life's purpose; for personal reflection and effective decision-making. We also provide a proven personal strategic planning method.

We hope the insights, stories and activities challenge and inspire you to take risks that lead to personal growth, and that they help you on your way to *success with soul*.

The stories in this book are drawn from a range of situations and people with whom we have come into contact over many years. While some stories are about specific individuals, others are based on the combined experiences of a number of people.

Finally, the book is co-authored and the views expressed reflect the joint opinions of both authors.

We hope you enjoy *Success With Soul*.

Doris Pozzi and Stephen Williams

Acknowledgments

The development of this book has been a long journey and a huge learning experience for us. Many contributors have added to this learning experience along the way. Their positive energy is here on these pages. Some deserve special mention: Lesley Thwaites, our publishing consultant, for her professionalism, energy and enthusiasm all along the journey; the team at Dorian Welles, including Leaellyn Rich for her hard work, Danielle Doss, and Lynne Clark for her persistent work in chasing down references and her work on the figures; Cathy Smith for her perseverance and professional editing; Evelyn Scannell and Monash University for providing much of the background research material on personal values (we hope we have done it justice); Paul Kenny for providing just the right kind of positive enthusiasm when it was needed at the front end of the project; Terry Sherf, our US publishing consultant for her timely advice and good, hard common sense; the team at Marcus Lee Design for their cover design work and Robert Klinkhamer for designing the text and putting it all together; Chris O'Connor for helping to clarify our thinking on the soul and for sharpening the text. Also, thanks to Dave Kreimer, Art Merrick, Glenn Ostrager, Michael and Nazih Dib, Fred Searls, Michael Dougherty, Dan Poynter and Paul Montgomery.

We would also like to thank our readers, who included Errol Muir, Barry Deane, John McCahon, Michael Wedd, John Daniliec, Rod Harris, Paul Kenny, Kate Gorham, Margaret Taylor, Jamie and Tracey Johnson, Owen Salter and Melissa Mackey.

We are grateful to our many clients whose experiences we have drawn on and who have shaped the direction of the book, and for their patience as we struggled to manage the tension between the book and our work for them; and to our many friends and colleagues at the Institute of Cultural Affairs (ICA) for their assistance and ideas, in particular John Burbidge, Bruce Robertson, and Phil Dowsett. Without them there would be no book. Thanks also go to The Epoch Foundation for all their enthusiasm and support.

A very special thank you to Edward Eckhardt, for over ten years of encouragement and belief in our abilities.

For the contributors we have not mentioned, we hope you see your valued contribution on the pages of *Success With Soul*.

Doris Pozzi and Stephen Williams

INTRODUCTION

THE CURRENT FEELING

INTEGRATING THE SUCCESSFUL SIDE of our lives with the side concerned with meaning – the soulful – is one of the key issues we struggle with today. Many of us have worked long and hard at careers that have provided many good things – recognition, money and comfortable lifestyles – but for some reason we still feel unsatisfied. We have come to a point where we know we could go further, but don't know how. Somehow our lives are lacking. We ask ourselves, could this be all that life has to offer?

The African Kikuyus use a special phrase to describe why they periodically go into the bush to be alone. It is to "let their souls catch up with their bodies". We, too, need to let our souls catch up with our bodies.

Psychologists and counsellors see thousands of clients each week who exhibit unclassifiable maladies. These maladies are variously described as vague depression, disillusionment, meaninglessness and lack of fulfillment. These problems persist despite hard work to solve them. And many of us do work hard – balancing commitments of time and money, family and work; trying to exercise, maintain a proper diet, get enough sleep and not get overly stressed, while holding down demanding jobs or maybe coping with having no job at all.

The burden falls on everyone – men and women, young and old. We feel the pressure to balance these competing commitments – to live a *balanced lifestyle*.

Doris used to work with an "expert balancer". Julie, a manager in the marketing department of a large consumer goods company, had the office down the corridor from hers. She was thirty-seven years old at the time, married with two young children. Julie's husband also worked full time, for a large management consulting company.

Julie was always busy – meetings to go to, business trips to take and seminars to attend – rushing past Doris's office many times a day. She worked hard to get ahead and be successful.

Like many of us, Julie was not just interested in being successful at work. She wanted to be successful outside work, too. Among other things, she wanted to be a successful parent and a successful partner.

Julie was also one of the office's good listeners, so there was always a stream of people coming to her office to talk. She often became involved in listening to and solving other people's problems. Everyone wanted a piece of her time.

Doris also used to go into Julie's office to talk. She always found Julie looking tired and run off her feet. If Doris suggested that she should slow down, she'd agree, and that too would be added to her long list of things to do. The fact was that Julie was trying to do too many things, trying to "balance" too many commitments.

With her energy always low, a personally satisfying performance in any of her roles was difficult. At the office, her work was always good but rarely creative. Her children, while generally well-behaved, were often uptight and temperamental. Her husband worried about her a great deal.

How did Julie run her life? She focused on the next thing on her "to do" list, the next urgent problem at work or home or the next person to walk through her office door. Julie was spread around pretty thin. There was no time left for Julie; certainly none left for her soul.

So many demands seem to be coming at us from all directions – from bosses, work colleagues, friends, families and even from people we don't even personally know, through media and marketing messages. Often these demands are challenges to be "successful" in a whole range of areas. They are often compelling and frequently contradictory. Meanwhile, the world within us – the world of the soul – is being ignored.

But just what do we mean by "soul"? It is a word that seems to mean many things to many people. After all, we can listen to "soul" music, have a "soul" mate, tolerate difficult circumstances because they are "good for the soul", and we often describe a dead-end job as "soulless" or "soul destroy-ing". It is a word that people use in many different ways, but one for which they would be hard pressed to provide a simple definition.

For now, let's be content to say that, for our purposes, the soul is *that part of our non-physical being that is the home of real personal meaning*. Later in the book we take a brief look at the historical and cultural/religious background of this elusive but ever-present concept.

Although some people don't believe that the soul exists, for most of us the soul is something very real. The tragedy is that today we are often only aware of the soul because of its absence in our lives. We associate the soul with that hollow feeling we experience. It is something we yearn for – some-thing we miss.

Some people believe soul is something purely spiritual. They experience the soul in their relationship with God, their church and in prayer. But this belief does not totally protect them from the same problems everybody else has. Many of the issues don't go away. These people can still feel the same external pressures, as well as the tensions between their search for meaning and the drive for success and achievement.

The fact is that until very recently we stopped talking about this something called *the soul*. We have been out of touch with soul. We put it down somewhere like an extra parcel and continued our journey without it.

Perhaps, like many others today, you went through a period during the 1980s when work and career were everything. You put in long hours and reaped tangible rewards – status, recognition and money. In short, you gained the things we usually associate with "success". However, for many people, this kind of success came at a high price: health suffered, relationships suffered and ultimately, work also began to suffer. In the worst cases, people lost their jobs or their relationships broke up. Major personal transitions were required just to put things back together again. Many of us are still involved in this process.

Now we are starting to talk about soul again. We want to bring it back into our lives. In the 1960s, one way people tried to achieve this was by "dropping out". They turned their backs on the whole mainstream "success thing" and devoted themselves to the inner journey. In the 1990s though, we don't necessarily want to turn our backs on everything and go sit on the top of a mountain to rediscover our souls. (Well, maybe for a little while, but not permanently.)

There are many good things in our current lives that we want to retain. The "drop everything" or "drop out" approaches no longer seem to be the answer. We don't want to give up the successful parts of our lives to achieve the soulful. We want both – success with soul.

In fact, a key issue we face today is how we will resolve the tension between success and soul. How we deal with that issue has enormous implications, not only for each of us personally, but for our societies and for the globe. In many ways, success and soul lie at the heart of issues such as environmental and economic sustainability.

The fact is that many people today have already come a long way down the path of personal growth. Over the past few decades, our communication skills have improved, we have developed time-management skills and learned a great deal about the role of personality, among other things. Now we have to continue that journey.

> In the '60s we tried to change the world, in the '70s we tried to change ourselves, and in the '80s we said, "Forget it, just give me the money."

With the pain and wisdom of past lessons, we are again seeking soul in our lives. This time around we know it is not just a case of rejecting everything in our current lives. We want to keep some aspects of the "success principle". However, we know the time has come to build change on the right foundations and principles.

ONE COMMON RESPONSE

Over the past few years a popular belief has developed that these issues of success and soul could be addressed *through achieving balance in our lives*. Our problems were caused by the fact that our lives were "unbalanced". "That must be it. I need to get a more balanced lifestyle." We have heard many of our friends say this. We have probably said it ourselves.

And it seems to make sense – just wind back some activities and contribute a bit more to others. Less time at work and more time at home. Less time at the bar and more time at the gym. "It's about time-management and planning," you say. "By taking better control of my *time* I will gain better control of my *life*." This sounds logical and seems like a fairly straightforward task.

So you fit in those things that you know you "should" be doing – regular exercise, a better diet, quality time with family, maybe a hobby. You do a course on time-management and begin to use your diary more frequently. You make lists – lots of lists – and find ways to use time more creatively.

We remember thinking the same things. If we could balance everything in our lives then we would be both successful and happy – jobs with regular hours, some leisure, time with the family, exercise, good diet and enough money. It would take some effort to achieve this balanced lifestyle but it could be done. We managed to do it. However, once we had, it turned out to be completely unsatisfying. It was hollow. It was like a drink that looks refreshing...until you drink it and find that it doesn't quench your thirst. And this was surprising and frustrating. We wondered why.

Many people we have spoken to on the issue of a balanced lifestyle have expressed the same frustration and dissatisfaction with this approach. They feel tired, dissatisfied, unfulfilled and, most of all, overcommitted. It all seems so hard to maintain and when they fail to meet their balanced lifestyle commitments, they feel guilty. The whole approach is inflexible and needs constant monitoring, often on a daily basis.

And what happens when we adopt a balanced lifestyle as the solution? Bosses and work colleagues put pressure on us when we cut down our work hours to "balance" our lives. Those less concerned about balance begin doing better than we are and we feel we are slipping behind. We still feel stressed and trapped. Important work and relationship issues always seem to require more time and energy than a balanced lifestyle affords. Our personal relationships may suffer, despite the "quality time" we put in.

Even the most successful "balancers" have problems. They may have achieved things like better health, better time-management skills and greater creativity. But many have still not addressed the issue of soul. After all, soul is not an activity or a commitment. It cannot be scheduled or planned. Like oil and water, balance and soul don't seem to mix properly.

Clearly there are many problems with these newly balanced lifestyles. A balanced lifestyle is simply not the whole story.

If we have it wrong now, what does history have to teach us about issues like balance, success and soul?

From pondering this question, one thought that comes to mind is: *the greatest human achievements have nothing to do with a balanced lifestyle at all*. In fact, they have often meant the opposite, involving individuals or groups of people working long, hard hours, day after day, for months and sometimes years on end. They certainly involved characteristics like confidence, perseverance and commitment. But balance? No, precious little of that. There are many examples, but let's look at one many of us will be familiar with.

THE STORY OF MICHELANGELO

Michelangelo was commissioned by Pope Julius II to paint a great work of art on the enormous, vaulted ceiling of the Sistine Chapel in the Vatican. The commission involved developing thousands of sketches, preparing the surface of the huge ceiling, grinding and mixing the paint colors and then applying them with sometimes giant brushstrokes overhead.

Although it was a huge undertaking, Michelangelo preferred to work alone. He did not even want someone else to grind and mix the colors for him. The work was dangerous, high above the ground on thin, wooden scaffolding. A fall would certainly have killed him.

Often he did not go out in the evening, not even to go home. At meal times the servant would climb the scaffolding to bring him some bread and a bowl of soup. He rested his arms and his eyes by meditating or writing verse, some of it comic. When he was overcome by tiredness he slept in his clothes with his boots on.

It was a method of working that would have deformed or crippled a man who did not have Michelangelo's muscles and nerves. He lay flat on his back, working day after day, month after month, year after year. His eyes strained upwards, his neck contracted, his spine pushed up against his stomach.

All the while, the Pope urged him to speed up progress on the work. The Pope was concerned that the ceiling would not be completed during his papal reign. Michelangelo would respond, "As soon as I can, Holy Father."

The entire work took four years to complete. When Michelangelo had finished the work he had almost lost his sight and walked with his head back, looking up. The personal toll on his body was enormous. Michelangelo had sacrificed his own health for a higher achievement – a creative act. At the expense of his body, he had vastly enriched his soul.

This certainly did not appear to be a balanced lifestyle. However, we would imagine that there was a great deal of personal satisfaction. And everyone would agree great success was achieved. It is also hard to believe that Michelangelo experienced the same feelings of hollowness and longing that many of us feel today.

Clearly, in Michelangelo's case, a balanced lifestyle did not contribute to achieving success with soul. Instead, success with soul came from a life that was very unbalanced for a period of time.

Success With Soul has been divided into three linked, but distinct, sections. The first part of the book presents a situational analysis of our current malaise, leading to a new, integrated way of thinking about success and soul. The second part presents activities, insights and methods to achieve personal success with real meaning. Finally, the last two chapters focus on how we live with this new reality where success and soul sit comfortably in our lives.

In this way, *Success With Soul* contains the wisdom, the knowledge and the know-how to move forward.

KNOWING

KNOWING

CHAPTER ONE

UNDERSTANDING
SUCCESS AND SOUL

THE WORD "SUCCESS" appears constantly in a range of areas including business self-help and personal growth literature. It often appears in the titles of books. There is even a business magazine called *Success*.

"Success" carries strong positive connotations. We like to use the word to evaluate people, objects and processes. We strive to achieve success. In a broad sense we wish to be successful.

And you may ask yourself
What is that beautiful house?
And you may ask yourself
Where does that highway go to?
And you may ask yourself
Am I right? ... Am I wrong?
And you may say to yourself
My God! ... What have I done?

David Byrne and Brian Eno

"Soul", on the other hand, has had a mixed history. This is partly because it is an abstract concept, hard to describe in words. Unlike success, a simple definition of soul does not just roll off the tongue. Moreover, "soul" appears to mean a lot of different things to different people. It seems to be part philosophical, part spiritual and part psychological.

Talking about soul raises questions about its relationship to other issues – issues like success. Many of us are now wondering, "How do I achieve success *and* soul in my life?" and "How do I balance the successful *and* soulful elements in my life?'

And why is this important? Why do we need to consider the relationship between success and soul? It is important because *we strive for success but we also crave soul*. Being successful relates directly to our motivation to achieve, while soul gives our lives meaning. For many of us, integrating success with soul (achievement with meaning) is therefore a central dynamic in our lives. For others, it may become important as a result of a significant event or milestone in our lives, such as turning forty.

A TRADITIONAL DEFINITION OF SUCCESS

If you had asked someone twenty years ago to define success, a common response would have been: "Success is what I want to achieve in my career. Success is a big house, a good job and lots of money."

This kind of success is measured by our *personal power, money, position and status*. These are the achievements or accomplishments of work; what many people seek to obtain when they leave for the office in the morning.

Sometimes we evaluate this kind of success using only one of these measures, for example our monthly salary or our job title. Sometimes we use a combination of these measures, such as our influence and position in politics.

Many people still think about success in this way. *The Fortune Top 500* and the *Forbes 400* richest people along with other lists of the rich, famous and powerful use these measures. And, when the media portray events in terms of winners (the successful) and losers (the unsuccessful), they are often using this model.

This traditional definition of success is a very powerful model. It has tangible measures and therefore provides an easy method of comparing people's relative success. But when we use this definition, what are we *really* saying about success?

Success, in this traditional definition, is often *externally defined*. Family, friends and society send us the message that we should strive to be successful, and often define the *type of success we should strive to achieve.* Some examples of the external messages we receive about success are that we should "have a top-level management career", "work in a prestigious industry", "be influential", "have a large salary", "be in great physical shape", "be attractive", "be sophisticated", "have impeccable academic qualifications from a top institution", "have a beautiful house", "have a wonderful partner", "have intelligent, beautiful children", etc., etc., etc. These are the achievements sought in this traditional definition of success. They relate to our personal power, money, position and status.

There is also a tendency in our society to grant authoritative status to voices or messages that are pervasive or popular. So we often accept persistent external messages, such as those from companies advertising products, and from political parties, interest groups and the media, that we should think or act in particular ways. Often these messages represent this traditional definition of success.

However, these external messages about success are also often contradictory. We are told we should have a successful career or business – which often entails spending long hours at work – *but* we "should" spend more time with the family. We are told we need to eat well to be healthy, but our "successful" lifestyles often preclude being able to do this.

The problem is that to do everything we are told we should do would require unlimited, and mostly unrealistic, amounts of money, time, energy, intelligence, commitment and ability. This is not possible for most people. What can happen in reality is an endless whirlwind of meaningless activity and effort. Instead of feeling successful, the individual is left feeling worn out and still personally unfulfilled.

While we may choose the area in which we wish to be "successful", success in this traditional definition exists and makes sense only in relation to significant others. To achieve this kind of success, *recognition* is required. You are recognized as being successful *by others*. Success is bestowed upon you. External recognition of success may come from a range of *sources*, for example from peers, family and friends, work colleagues, your boss or the general public.

As well as coming from a range of sources, recognition comes for different achievements – *recognition for hard work* ("Boy, he really worked hard on that"), *for mastery* ("That's an excellent picture she's painted"), *for competition* ("He's won every race in the past six months") and *for gaining rewards* ("She really made big dollars").

Generally we seek different types of recognition from different sources. We may want recognition for our mastery from our peers. We want rewards and recognition for our hard work from the boss. *To be successful we want the right types of recognition from the right sources.*

One of the reasons we strive for recognition is that recognition for being successful boosts our *self-esteem*. It makes us feel better about ourselves. However, we may not even recognize just how much this drives us to be successful.

> At school, Stephen often found it difficult to make friends. The children with lots of friends were usually the ones who were good academically or at sports, art or drama. He was not very good at any of these pursuits and this tended to lower his self-esteem. As a result, getting recognition – any recognition – was always very important. "I wanted to be successful at something – anything. I needed to be recognized. Performing well at sport or academically, *and then* not getting any recognition, was always worse than not doing well at all."

When we view success in these terms, success is about *competition with others*. To be successful we must win, and that means beating someone else. Winning may involve developing a better career or business, making more money, getting a more powerful job, being in better physical shape or achieving higher marks.

Competition shapes all of us to some extent, although for some people it may hardly be a motivator at all. However, in the traditional view of success, competition is a key factor.

So what does it mean if competition is an *intrinsic* element of success, if it virtually defines success? What are the implications? To begin with, if a vital element of success is competition, then success cannot exist in the absence of other people; in particular, other people who value the same sort of success we are trying to achieve. This means we must *measure our success against other people*. Other people are the yard-stick. We use their success to measure our own. In this view of success, success cannot exist without others against whom we can compete.

And who are we likely to be in competition with? Generally, people just like us – *people in our own league*. When we compete against someone, we tend to pick someone we have a chance of beating and someone there is some satisfaction in beating. Generally this someone will be next to us or just in front of us. For example, if we view success as having lots of money, we are not going to compete with the Sultan of Brunei. He has more money than we will ever have! Instead we compete with those around us – our families and friends, our work colleagues.

A company Stephen used to work for entered a running team in an inter-office Corporate Cup. The Corporate Cup was held over several months with a series of weekly time trials around a three-mile course. Many companies entered teams in the Cup. Points were awarded to the team based on the individual team members' overall times and their improvement over successive trials. The scoring system was designed to ensure runners principally competed against their own previous time.

Hanging over the start–finish line was a large digital clock. Runners would select a time to start and write it on the score sheets located near the start–finish line. As the clock ticked over to their chosen start time the runner commenced running. The circuit wandered along a river, then around a large park and back to the start–finish line. When the runners re-crossed the line they read the finish time on the digital clock and entered it on the score sheets.

It was an honor system, with each runner running their own race. Nonetheless, faster runners would often focus on the slower runners in front of them to improve their performance. They would push themselves to pass a slower runner. Once passed, another slower runner would be selected to catch.

In this form of competitive drive – a conscious decision to race against someone just in front of us – we are using someone else's performance to improve our own. Competition can be an effective tool for doing this.

But sometimes this competitive drive is not conscious. It is subconscious – we are not fully aware of what is motivating us to be successful. *Defining success in terms of our personal power, money, position or status often creates (conscious or subconscious) competition with others.* Competition with others, particularly when it is not fully conscious, can be very damaging to our relationships, including our relationships with people we work with, our friends, our families. This type of success demands competition, yet competitiveness can erode relationships.

Families can provide a person with many good things – a support network in times of trouble, a shoulder to cry on in times of sadness and a set of relationships where one can be accepted and loved no matter what one has or has not achieved. In short, families can provide us with unconditional love. They love us for ourselves and have a genuine desire to see us succeed and be happy.

However, this is not always the case. In some families, family members, consciously or subconsciously, choose to compete with one another. Ultimately, this can hurt the family by damaging the relationships within it. One person may seek to be successful by comparison with others in their family, but this competition can erode those very relationships that can have such a power to love, nurture and support.

Providing that competition is compartmentalized into specific areas of our lives it is not necessarily destructive. For example, two professional swimmers may compete strongly in the pool. However, out of the pool they may respect each other's talents and may even be the best of friends. Competition in families is rarely like this. It is often all-pervading, including how we are doing at work, in our relationships, financially or how we are bringing up our children – in short, our whole lives. Once this is the case, the good things that can come with family life, such as the opportunity for intimacy, are diminished.

Success defined in terms of competition is exclusive of others rather than inclusive. It says, "I want to emphasize the difference between us (to my advantage)", not "I value what we have in common as well as what makes you unique and special."

Also, if success is defined in terms of personal power, money, position and status, *we can always be more successful*. We can always have more of each of these things. Like the runner in the Corporate Cup, there is always someone else in front of us to pass; someone richer, more powerful, more experienced or more attractive.

In fact, we can always crave more success. This is the success treadmill. It's like we are on an exercise treadmill. The faster we run to accumulate success, the faster the treadmill turns. We expend a lot of energy but really go nowhere. Being on the success treadmill can really drive people.

Doris used to work for a company where the owner was on the success treadmill. Mary came from a family of business people. Mary's father Bill owned a chain of supermarkets and was very wealthy. Mary was always being told by Bill about how he had built the company up from nothing.

When Mary started her own business she would work long hours, seven days a week. She would regularly work all night to complete reports for the company's clients. Mary was a tenacious worker and was determined to make the company a success. Nothing would stand in her way.

And it *was* a success. Soon her business employed two staff, then three and then four. Quickly it grew out of Mary's small suburban office into a large downtown office with twenty full-time staff. Mary would drive her staff relentlessly. Some of them suffered "burn out" and a number left with bad feelings.

Even once the business was financially secure she continued to push her staff and herself relentlessly. Soon she began planning to open an interstate office and employ more staff.

But Mary didn't appear to be happier or more satisfied no matter how big the company grew. She simply continued to be driven to achieve higher turnover and to employ more and more staff.

This is sometimes the case with people on the success treadmill. While their company, their salary or their turnover continues to grow, they do not appear to be any more fulfilled or happy. What is happening here?

One of the dynamics may be that the individual is seeking success to fulfill another need. Their motivation to achieve ever-increasing success may come from insecurity or low self-esteem. They may be subconsciously seeking the love and recognition of a parent or partner. Sometimes parents unwittingly convey the message that love is conditional on a child's success and achievement. Often what the parents really mean is that they want their child to succeed for the child's own sake. But the child may then be motivated to seek personal success to gain the parental love that should be theirs unconditionally.

> I like obsessive people –
> they get things done!
>
> *Edina* – Absolutely Fabulous

This is one of the problems with seeing success in terms of material achievements. There is always the danger of its pursuit becoming obsessive or driven by insidious subconscious forces. However, even when it is not, it can leave people feeling unfulfilled or unhappy.

The traditional definition of success is about achievement. So, what drives people to seek this kind of success? In the 1980s, psychologists Janet Spence and Robert Helmreich conducted research on achievement motivators. They found that there are three key motivations to achieve. These are the *desire to work hard, striving for mastery* and *competitiveness*. We might perhaps add a fourth – *rewards*. In trying to understand what success is for us it can be helpful to think about what motivates us to achieve. The following stories illustrate these different motivations.

Ben works long hours and really puts in at the office. He talks constantly about the amount of work he does. His achievement motivation is focused on his desire to work hard and he rarely talks about how well his career is progressing. Ben hasn't had a promotion in many years and doesn't care. He does not even seem to mind when someone else is promoted above him. His work is mainly clerical and he does it competently but rarely outstandingly.

Andrew is an artist. He works hard at his art and is trying to master the techniques required to make great art. He is not competitive. Andrew doesn't care how well he is doing relative to his fellow artists. Andrew sees achievement in terms of working hard and personal mastery of technique and expression.

Sue works long hours in her job in the finance industry. At the end of the day, she works out at the gym, spending an hour or so there most days. She is keen to develop her knowledge of fitness, as well as staying fit. To that end she has studied all the muscle groups, including their names and what they do. On weekends, Sue sometimes does marathons and biathlons. Often she talks about how well she has performed relative to other people – both in her sports and at work. Finally, she also focuses on the rewards that her job brings – in particular, money, travel, executive "toys" and promotions. Sue is very competitive. All four dimensions of achievement are part of Sue's outlook on life and success.

Finally, when we operate out of this model of success, we often see success as applying to a *part* of our lives rather than to our whole lives. This traditional definition of success often relates to that area of our lives that might be called our business, career, vocation or work. It may be our trade, profession or a major field of personal endeavor.

When we think about success in this way, it invariably leads to an individual's "worth" being measured by their power, money or status. Those individuals without the trappings of success are seen as failures, even if they have other kinds of success. We see the side effects of this in the low sense of self-worth that unemployed people can have of themselves, or in the low status of the "housewife" in some societies today.

So, in overview, this traditional view of success is about *achievement*, particularly achievement relative to others, and *competition* is a strong driver for this type of success.

Since the 1950s, a different view of success has developed. The focus and drivers behind this new type of success are different, as are the goals being sought. We might call this more recent popular view of success a modern definition.

A MODERN DEFINITION OF SUCCESS

Another increasingly popular definition of success is success as *the pursuit of excellence and personal fulfillment*. This definition is about being true to yourself and making the most of your talents. In sporting terms, it *is about being your best*. The pursuit of excellence and personal fulfillment is seen as the key to personal satisfaction, happiness and peace of mind.

This kind of success can be achieved without concern for recognition. Recognition may be a pleasant side effect of our personal success, but it is not necessarily the key motivator. The individual is motivated from within, motivated by their interest in personal excellence and fulfillment.

Our friend Peter is not particularly impressive when other people meet him. He is very modest about his achievements and is a better listener than talker, especially when it comes to talking about himself. What Peter *is* interested in is developing his mind. He finished a degree in the humanities fifteen years ago and has been studying in a range of areas ever since. As a result he has a good grasp of areas as disparate as history, psychology and law. Peter doesn't seek recognition for his knowledge or academic achievements. He is focused on developing his mind as far as he can.

This modern definition of success – the pursuit of excellence and personal fulfillment – is not necessarily about competition with others. We don't have to compete against anyone else to be our best. The competition is internal – the inner game of success, if you like.

Unlike the traditional definition, where there are clear, tangible goals (often defined by others), this definition of success does not tell us in any detail what we should do to achieve success. This is up to the individual to decide. We must make our own path and define our own achievements or goals to achieve personal success.

How do we define success for ourselves? How do we find an answer? And is there only one answer? Could some answers be right and others wrong? Individuals have to answer a lot of questions for themselves when they see success as personal fulfillment and the pursuit of excellence.

This way of thinking about success also leaves the door open for some individuals to define success in ways others may believe is wrong, selfish, bad or evil. The advocates of this modern definition generally attempt to close this door by stating that although individuals can define success for themselves, they must do so within the framework of ethics, morality and principles.

Those who accept that their definition of personal success should fit within this framework have a number of options. They are to:
• seek the assistance of experts in ethics
• defer to an authority such as a religion, philosophy or the law
• use their consciences for guidance, or
• consult a number of these sources for assistance.

This is a central dilemma of our "anything goes" post-modern era. It is up to the individual to decide what framework he or she will work within, if any. Some people do hold strong beliefs which direct this behavior. The reality for many of us, though, is that at some point we choose to follow a particular path, but then internal and external forces push us back to the "path of least resistance". For example, we may take on vegetarianism for a while, but then float back to our usual habits. We take up regular exercise, then heavy work schedules push it out of our routine again. Or we begin to recycle our garbage, but as it requires extra effort, we slowly return to doing what is easier.

This definition also does not explicitly include soul. How the soul fits into this view of success is not clear. If we wish to integrate success and soul some added clarification is required.

This modern definition also says nothing about relationships – it focuses on the individual. Personal fulfillment is just that – *personal*. Relationships are not necessarily considered important for personal fulfillment.

The fact is that none of the current, prevalent definitions of success is wholly satisfactory if we wish to achieve success with real meaning. The other fact is that a new definition of success is starting to emerge.

Before going on to describe this view of success that is just now beginning to emerge, it is time to turn our attention from past and recent definitions of success to the views of the soul throughout history.

How has soul been defined in the past?

Centuries ago, our ancestors ventured deep into dark caves to paint images of animals such as bison and deer. Why? Was it part of a ritual to capture the soul of the animal, or was it celebrating a successful hunting trip? Perhaps the paintings formed part of an initiation or rite-of-passage ceremony. We will never know for sure. However, we do know that there was symbolic significance in these paintings. They were not purely decorative. When we look at these paintings today, it is hard to believe our ancestors were not also thinking about the soul.

Today, some ancient cultures, such as the Native Americans and the Australian Aboriginal people, consider their souls to be within other animals, in trees and the earth. Some people are considered to have more than one soul. They may also be part of a collective or communal soul along with animals, plants or the land.

All cultures refer to the soul, and while words and abstractions may vary, the concept of the soul is universal. In many ways, it seems that the concept of the soul has developed to answer those persistent questions: Why are we alive? What makes us who we are?

EARLY WRITINGS ON THE SOUL

Our models of the human soul have evolved over time, beginning many centuries ago. The earliest known writings on the soul are by the ancient Egyptians, who believed that the soul forms part of the Gnostic Myth of the creation. According to this myth, God laughed six times and created the Gods of light, water, alchemy, fate, time and power. On the seventh and final laugh, however, God cried at the same time and as a result the soul was created.

The writings of the Ancient Greeks on the soul are extensive. Philosophers such as Aristotle and Plato developed many of the fundamental ideas on the soul. Aristotle described the soul as that which makes all things live – *the animating principle*. He also believed that the soul was something distinct and different from the body. Plato asserted that each individual soul is *immortal* and that the soul exists before and after the existence of the body. Death therefore releases the soul and, in this way, the soul links us to the afterlife.

However, some classical scholars, such as the Jewish philosopher Philo Judaeus, spoke of the *duality of the soul*; the irrational (soul-breath) and rational (soul-shadow) soul. The irrational soul is believed to expire at death, while the rational soul is immortal.

CULTURE, RELIGION AND THE SOUL

There is no single Christian view on the soul; rather there are a number of different views derived from Eastern and Western religious traditions. The Old Testament takes a Western view, that the soul is that which makes a living being. This is described in Genesis. The soul is the breath of God creating life from the inanimate earth. In these scriptures, the soul is seen as the *person's true identity*. It is the whole person or the whole *person*-ality.

An alternative Christian concept of the soul deriving from an Eastern religious perspective is that *God and creation are synonymous*. In this way, we are enclosed in the creative act, not separate entities with souls.

Many Christian theologians believe the soul is important as a metaphor which helps us understand our relationship with God. The soul is an element of the spiritual dimension; it connects us to God. The thirteenth-century Christian philosopher, St Thomas Aquinas, describes the indestructibility of the soul. This characteristic of the person's soul or *spirit* allows it to ascend to heaven (or descend to hell) after death.

Most Eastern cultures honor the soul in their teachings. Judaism and Islam support the view that the soul is created by God. The soul is mentioned in the creation stories of both these faiths. Islamic texts state that the souls of the faithful are transformed into white birds which reside with Allah in heaven. Hindu teachings also describe the soul and its immortality. The Hindu scripture, the Bhagavad Gita, states that "the soul is perceived in a pure and serene mind in the act of introspection and intuition". Devout acts are seen as part of the *purification of the soul.*

Throughout all of these spiritual or religious views of the soul, three distinct themes seem to exist. They are the soul as the totality of the personality or the self, the soul as the life force or the spirit, and the soul connecting us to other living creatures and our surroundings.

Religious practices, rites and rituals were often seen as "feeding the soul". For example, ancient initiation rituals, games and religious ceremonies exposed the mystery and power of the soul. Symbolism often played an important role, with objects, such as paintings, totems, costumes and masks, representing the soul of an animal or ancestor or the universal soul. These basic themes and concepts still pervade many religious traditions today, for example the breaking of bread and drinking of wine in the Christian sacrament of Communion.

PHILOSOPHY, PSYCHOLOGY AND THE SOUL

Through the centuries, philosophers have continued to consider the existence and nature of the soul. The fifteenth-century Italian philosopher and physician Marsilio Ficino saw the soul as immortal and believed that it had an important role in *the search for truth*, whereas the French Renaissance philosopher René Descartes suggested that the *soul is joined to the whole body*, and is principally seated in a small gland (the pineal gland) in the brain. This concept, described as the "the ghost in the machine", was also supported by Italian philosopher Giordano Bruno. In the 1600s, scientific psychologist Baruch Spinoza rejected the concept of a separate soul, believing the soul to be *inherent in the mind*. Spinoza also went on to suggest that the mind (soul) is immortal and continues to exist after death.

German philosopher Gottfried Leibnitz argued that the soul is a *monad* or *indivisible unit of being*. Leibnitz believed that the quest of the soul was self-knowledge. Another German philosopher, Immanuel Kant, believed the soul was one of the unconditional truths. In this sense, the soul was seen as a *thought* and was connected to the concept of moral law. In Georg Hegel's book *Philosophy of Mind*, this concept was explored further when he proposed that the soul is not a thing, but a process. Later, the twentieth-century German existentialist Karl Jaspers defined the soul or *subconscious*, along with matter, life and spirit, as one of the four states of being.

Soul has also been used as a psychological term. In fact the word "psychotherapy" derives from the Greek and literally means "healing the soul". Italian Renaissance physicians and counsellors like Marsilio Ficino saw part of their role as caring for the souls of their patients, not solely ministering to the body.

More recently, Carl Jung, the famous twentieth-century psychologist, studied both the mind and the soul. Jungian psychology links the soul or "anima" with the subconscious. Jung's theories on human development are, in part, theories on the journey of the soul. He also conceptualized relationships as being, at a deeper level, a dialogue between souls. These later concepts of the soul continued the process of refining the notion of soul in terms of science and the mind. This process has recast the soul's initial explanation and, in some ways, reduced its symbolic importance.

ART AND THE SOUL

Soul is encoded in art and translated by the viewer.

The soul has an important symbolic power for artists and writers. Poets such as John Keats and Walt Whitman have been inspired and fascinated by the soul, while William Shakespeare and Robert Browning have used the power of the soul to evoke romantic love, spiritual love, inner strength or events of mythological significance.

Rembrandt's self-portraits have been interpreted as a "psychoanalysis of his soul". Renaissance artists' exploration of science, mythology and the human condition is, in part, an exploration of soul. Landscape painting, ranging from Brueghel's depictions of the seasons through to Turner's atmospheric scenes and works by Australian Aboriginal painters, map the soul in nature and in the land in many different ways.

The soul and spirituality have also been explored by abstract artists. Islamic art uses patterning to symbolize God's glory. The painter Mark Rothko used massive abstract paintings to evoke a "spiritual presence".

Soul can be found at the intersection of spirituality, love and art.

The soul has romantic and emotional significance. It conveys a sense of depth, love and power. Romantic love is often described as the "mixing of souls". Love and the soul (Eros and Psyche) comprise a seminal theme in literature and painting. The great allegorical paintings of Renaissance and Mannerist artists Titian, Bronzino and Veronese blend love and the soul with mythological stories. In *Portrait of the Artist as a Young Man*, James Joyce describes love as the "outburst of profane joy" in the soul of the young hero, Stephen Dedalus.

THEN SOUL WENT MISSING

In the twentieth century, soul gradually receded from Western thought. The steady rise of the social sciences and the evolution of theology tended to phase out the soul. With the triumph of materialism, the soul's intangibility also contributed to its own decline.

The word "soul" resurfaced from time to time. It was appropriated in the 1960s by African-Americans, who gave it a new meaning. Soul was about brotherhood, freedom and civil rights. There was soul food, soul music and soul power.

Soul was part of a social movement rather than an inherent foundation of individual personality.

Mainstream psychology has tended to down-play the notion of soul, particularly the religious and spiritual elements. In areas where psychology has focused on measurement, and not meaning, the soul rarely rates a mention.

Twentieth-century psychology has emphasized scientific, mechanistic approaches rather than approaches that are more hermeneutical; that is, approaches that elucidate the "meaning" behind human actions. The soul cannot be measured, so modern psychology hasn't wanted to know about it. The soul's boundaries have been considered too diffuse to allow identification and acceptance within this medical model of psychology. A relatively small number of psychologists and social scientists have seen the role of their disciplines as hermeneutical. In this approach, the soul has a place.

> American psychology seems to have lost its soul.
>
> *Michael R. Jackson*

Theologians also seemed to have more or less dismissed the concept of soul. More recent revisions of biblical texts have tended to substitute or delete references to the word. A comparison of the King James Version and the New Revised Standard Version of the Bible illustrates this shift; "soul" became "body", "life" or "person", or was removed entirely.

In Western society, the gradual decline of organized religion has also turned attention away from the soul. Many people's interest in faith and spirituality has declined, and with it people's interest in the soul. In this century, these occurrences led to a type of "dark ages" for the concept of soul.

THE SOUL RETURNS

Towards the end of the 1980s, the effects of the stockmarket crash and worldwide recession were felt in many people's lives. At the same time we experienced downsizing by corporations, increased personal stress and, along with it, some fundamental questioning of our place in the world. Other developments, such as increasing environmental concerns and the decreasing faith in many forms of psychotherapy, also added to the malaise. Out of this turmoil, the soul has recently re-emerged.

Contemporary writers such as Phil Cousineau, Thomas Moore, Jack Canfield and Mark Victor Hansen have been drawing on the soul for inspiration. Thomas Moore describes soul as a "quality or dimension of experiencing life and ourselves". Dr Tian Dayton and Jack Canfield describe our connection with soul through everyday experience. Recent writings on the soul are drawing together psychology and spirituality. Ideas and concepts based on the soul, deriving from early sources such as Plotinus, Marsilio Ficino and the Greek philosophers, are being reinterpreted to address contemporary issues.

The word "soul" is returning to usage in our everyday language. Even the rise of environmentalism can be seen as a rebirth of the concept of a universal soul. We are starting to talk and think about soul again. Issues such as "caring for the soul" and "finding your soul mate" have brought the soul back into our consciousness. Through this renaissance, the concept of soul has received broader interpretations than its previously specific and religious ones.

When we talk about soul in this book, we are focusing on *that dimension of ourselves concerned with meaning*. Soul is about what is meaningful to us in our lives. This definition blends both spiritual and cognitive approaches to soul. Hence, success with soul is about success that is meaningful.

COMPARISON OF SUCCESS AND SOUL

So far we have considered a number of different views of success, and a range of views on the soul. Let us now bring these two concepts together and compare them. Understanding the similarities and differences between existing views of success and soul is the next step toward integrating the two. We need to become attuned to how each can reinforce or repel the other.

Both traditional and modern views of success are about focusing on the future or striving for something, such as improving oneself or achieving a goal. Conversely, soul is often found in the present. Previous models of success have also tended to encourage self-admiration, self-aggrandizement and hubris or pride, while soul emphasizes modesty and humility.

While success is often measured by competition with others, being better or different, our soul relates directly to our uniqueness and individuality; but it is also discovered in our relationships with others. So success is, in many ways, *exclusive*, whereas soul is *inclusive*.

Success has also been about acquisition, achievement and possession – this traditional view of success emphasizes change. Conversely, the soul is often described as immortal – soul therefore emphasizes continuity and permanence.

Traditional and modern definitions of success are about using our skills and talents. Success is gained through the desire to improve, and

> **Fame and tranquillity can never be bedfellows.**
>
> *Montaigne*

by striving to do so. Conversely, soul is about acknowledging who we are at a very fundamental level, and respecting that.

All of this suggests that success and soul, as they are popularly conceived, are irreconcilable. They exist at opposite ends of a spectrum. Is it any wonder that such a plague of emptiness and meaninglessness coexists with such high levels of wealth and success in our Western consumer society?

The fundamental differences between success and soul, as our society currently sees them, are so great that they seem to be mutually exclusive. Trying to reconcile success with soul as they are currently defined means attempting the juxtaposition of *hubris* (success) and *humility* (soul).

A new way of talking about success is needed. This new way must be one that considers the needs of the soul, a way that integrates the concepts of success and soul, a way that enables us to move forward with both.

The Eastern view of the world has a way of talking about integration – there doesn't have to be an *either/or* situation. We do not want a choice between success and soul. We desire a *both/and* resolution. We desire *both* to be unique and special *and* to belong. We need and seek success *and* soul.

Striving just for success fulfills only one fundamental human need – the need for achievement. Along the way we must also fulfill our need for soul. We require a new form of success that attends to soul. We need the meaning that soul creates. Therefore, to allow us to move forward and achieve success with soul, success must be redefined.

In this chapter we have discussed the ways in which, up to now, people have thought about success and soul. We have seen some of the limitations of the current ways in which success is defined. We have also discussed the development of our understanding of the soul. In the following chapter we will look at what we already know about living our lives, the wisdom we already have. This will then form the foundation on which we will build a new definition of success.

WHAT WE
ALREADY KNOW

> All experience is an arch to
> build upon.
>
> *Henry Brooks Adams*

T HE CURRENT UNDERSTANDING of personal growth is composed of both "ancient wisdom" and modern insights. That understanding has drawn deeply from the fields of psychology, philosophy, physics and sociology to name just a few. These fields have provided important insights in areas such as interpersonal communication, personality, creativity, health and planning.

The current wisdom includes "common sense" advice about eating properly, getting regular exercise and enough sleep. This advice still holds true. Nothing in recent research suggests that this has changed. Nobody has found a miracle cure for the effects of smoking, unhealthy diet or excessive alcohol consumption.

Recently, the synthesis of many diverse fields is increasing our understanding of how to be effective, successful and fulfilled human beings. As we move forward, however, it is important that we take the best of this wisdom with us. There is a strong tendency in our society to blindly replace the old with the new. Unfortunately, in doing so, we sometimes discard things that are valuable. It is like the old saying about throwing out the baby with the bath water.

So, before moving on, let's take a little time to reflect on some of the important knowledge that already exists.

SUCCESS BEGINS FROM WITHIN

Personal growth requires personal change; change that must start from within the individual. It must start with a person's values and attitudes.

Over many years, our company has been involved in many organizational change programs. These have included change programs to implement new technology, improve product quality, create a customer service culture, increase environmental awareness and improve safety performance. From our experience, all successful change programs share one thing in common – they all place a major emphasis on "the person". Conversely, unsuccessful change programs predominantly focus on variables outside the person, without sufficient consideration of the human element. They consider the technology, systems and processes in an organization, but not the people who have to interact with them.

Not only is it important to focus on people in organizational change, it is important to begin with what happens within people – their beliefs, values, attitudes and commitment. These provide the catalyst for effective organizational change.

It is the same with personal change. Personal change must start from within – examining our own attitudes, beliefs, values and commitment. Then, as we achieve change within ourselves, we can go on to achieve change outside ourselves. In his book *The Seven Habits of Highly Effective People*, Dr Stephen Covey describes this process as *"inside-out"*. It is the process of creating personal victories that lead to public victories.

We will take this concept a little further, first by drawing on new research about the way in which our personal values shape our attitudes and actions, and secondly by considering how our commitment and actions can, in turn, shape our attitudes and ultimately change our values. Finally, we will show how personal success can be redefined to incorporate both our personal and public victories and also help us to rediscover soul.

PERSONALITY IS NOT THE ANSWER

Considerable research and a large number of psychology books, both past and recent, have focused on personality as the key to success in life, to getting what we want and influencing others. A substantial body of management literature is based on this view. People are categorized into personality types so that, for example, they can be better "managed" and be turned into better managers. Dr Covey calls this approach *the personality ethic* and explains that after World War I, "Success became more a function of personality, of public image, of attitudes and behaviors, skills and techniques, that lubricate the processes of human interaction." This approach emphasizes skills such as human and public relations techniques and a positive mental attitude. It can also encourage potentially insidious techniques such as manipulation and intimidation.

This is not a completely negative picture. The psychology of personality has provided some benefits, for example, in understanding preferred modes of communication and different working styles. Insights into the psychology of personality have also been used successfully in marriage guidance, career consulting and for employee selection. Understanding our own personality and the personalities of others can be one way to modify our behavior and to make our interactions more successful.

Despite these benefits, the psychology of personality is not the answer. We all accept that people have different personalities and styles. We have all probably worked with someone with whom we "clash". However, when something is important enough, to all of us, we somehow still manage to achieve our goals, don't we?

Interdisciplinary project teams often comprise people with quite different personalities. Stephen has worked on a number of successful projects developing businesses from newly discovered mineral deposits. Here geologists, engineers, project managers, finance people, accountants and environmentalists work together to build a new business. The skills required to develop these complex projects successfully are many and varied. The personalities of those involved can also vary widely. While generalizations can be dangerous, Stephen found that geologists tended to be creative, optimistic and conceptual thinkers. Engineers were often more measured, conservative and interested in detail. Environmentalists were quite passionate about their discipline.

"Despite the broad range of personalities involved, these multidisciplinary teams regularly managed to achieve successful outcomes. The success of the teams was due to commitment, shared vision and values rather than the mastery of personality issues."

The fact is that a focus on personality fails to deliver when it comes to the most important issues. For instance, it provides very little assistance in defining and achieving personal success. It is even less helpful in issues relating to soul.

Why has the psychology of personality failed to deliver? It has failed because the reality is that personality only contributes a *very small part* of what it is to be human. Human behavior is more strongly driven by values, beliefs and character than by personality. Also, it has failed because personality often focuses on the differences that exist among us rather than those things we all have in common – like soul.

SOUL EXISTS AND IS RELEVANT

Recently, we have begun to recognize that rational, cognitive approaches to solving our psychological and social problems don't always work, that it is not always simply a question of "thinking" through problems. In fact, purely rational approaches can be counterproductive and ineffective. In moments of calm we may think through issues and find solutions – solutions that

> A timeless, limitless, perfect unity underlies all our feeling and thought, underlies every form of existence and every part of our self.
>
> *Karl Gustav Carus*

29

don't work when we try to implement them because of strong emotions and feelings that arise at that point. Similarly, our rational self may consider what is logical or rational but ignore what is meaningful.

> A few years ago we had to work through the issue of selling an old house. The house used to belong to an older member of Doris's family who had passed it on to us. The house was run down, needing extensive repairs, and lacked modern conveniences. It was basically pretty unlivable without some substantial attention. We didn't really have the time or the money to devote to this task. The logical decision was to sell it.
>
> But something stopped us doing it. There was a nagging feeling that it was the wrong thing to do. Many generations of Doris's family had lived in that house and it was the only tie with her heritage. The fact of the matter was that the house had soul, and the voice of soul stopped us selling it despite all rational considerations.

Important personal decisions often involve strong emotions and feelings. Decisions affecting our vocation, where we live, our family, children, partner or the environment, are often issues that involve more than rational thinking; they involve soul.

We are beginning to recognize that we need to get back in touch with this dimension of ourselves called soul. To an extent we are starting to rediscover soul.

WHERE THE MIND GOES THE BODY WILL FOLLOW

To achieve something, it must be created twice. First, it must be created in the mind; it must be visualized. Only then can it be created in form and realized in the world.

We create the future in our mind. This is the first step towards that new future. In other words, where the mind goes the body will follow. The following simple activity illustrates this principle.

Make a pendulum from some sort of weight, like a paper clip, and a piece of cotton thread. The thread should be about 10 inches (25 centimetres) long and the weight should swing freely.

On a sheet of paper draw a compass arrow with a circle around it. The diagram below is an example. Your circle should be about 2 inches (5 centimetres) across. Place the sheet of paper in front of you with the north arrow pointing away from you.

Rest your elbow on the table with the string in your hand. The weight should hang just above the centre of the compass point. Use your other hand at first to steady the string if you need to.

NORTH

SOUTH

Now, holding your hand and arm steady, concentrate on the weight. Visualize it moving in a north–south direction following the arrow head. Watch the pendulum closely and concentrate hard.

Notice after a few seconds how the pendulum begins to swing in the direction you visualized. By setting the simple goal of moving the pendulum, the body moves into action and suddenly, little by little, the pendulum begins to move. Even though you don't think *you* are moving the pendulum, it is happening. This is not a "psychic" phenomenon. Physical action is involved, but the action is initiated by the mind.

Many sporting people use visualization. They visualize their goals and give these goals positive energy.

We all know what happens when we don't set goals for ourselves. We can tend to drift along from day to day. On the other hand, with tangible goals and a clear vision of what we want to achieve, we tend to move towards that vision. In this way, the journey towards personal success starts with creating that vision in our minds.

Mental models underlie our thinking

Humans use *mental models* to conceptualize the world, our behavior and the environment. Mental models are structures of thinking which attempt to describe and predict. At the simplest level they are "ways of thinking about things". The different ways of thinking about success and soul that we explored in the last chapter are examples of mental models.

Mental models shape human action because they provide a *framework of understanding*. For example, when you drive a car you have a mental model about the way the car will behave in response to your instructions. When you turn the wheel to the left you expect the car to turn left. We predict this, and normally it is supported by fact. We do not understand all the mechanics – we don't have to. Our mental model provides sufficient understanding to drive the car successfully.

Mental models are often developed in one field, such as mathematics, physics, economics or psychology, to understand an aspect of that field. For example, mental models are used to understand the behavior of animals in groups, interactions between atoms, and among people in organizations.

A model from one field can be used to shed new light on a different field. For example, Jungian and Freudian concepts of the subconscious were incorporated into art in the 1920s with the development of techniques such as automatic writing and frottage. The model of a biological organism has been applied to our entire planet with the Gaia Principle, where the entire globe is seen as one single living organism. Mental models from organic biology have also been taken and applied to further the understanding of economics.

Mental models develop over time. For example, the mental model of the relationship between humans and their environment has changed significantly over time. The four main mental models for our relationship to the environment and the resultant social attitudes are shown below. Recent developments in environmental consciousness and concern for the planet have led to the most recent development of our mental model.

How we view our relationship to the environment

Period	Mental model	Resultant attitude
Pre-history	Competitive	"I compete for existence"
Agrarian	Exploitative	"I use the land"
Industrial	Manipulative	"I control the environment"
Post-industrial	Interdependent	"We are the caretakers of the planet"

CHAOS IS PART OF OUR LIVES

Often significant changes in mental models result in what is called a *paradigm shift*. For example, when humans went from seeing the earth as flat to seeing it as round, that was a paradigm shift – a fundamental shift in the way we saw the world. A recent paradigm shift occurred with the development of a new scientific model – chaos theory. Chaos theory is a term which encompasses a set of theories across a number of fields. Researchers in mathematics, meteorology and medical fields, among others, developed chaos theory from looking at a wide range of natural phenomena.

Chaos theory describes the behavior of non-linear systems. Non-linear systems include complex phenomena such as white water in a stream, the formation of natural landforms and the dripping of a water tap which goes from a steady pattern to a random one. Weather patterns, the growth of species populations and electrical activity in the heart can all display behavior which is described by chaos theory.

Chaotic systems have many attributes. One of these is that they can produce unpredictable outcomes from small variations in initial conditions. This is often described as the *butterfly effect*. The name derives from an example: the flapping of a butterfly's wings in Tokyo can affect the weather in Texas. The butterfly effect can be demonstrated by dropping two identical sticks into the same place in a turbulent stream. The sticks will initially follow the same path, but gradually diverge and end up in different locations. The butterfly effect makes long-range prediction of natural phenomena, such as the weather, extremely difficult.

Another attribute of chaotic systems is that they can display identical patterns at many different scales or levels. This *fractal patterning* is seen in the irregular shape of a coastline or the repetition of similar shapes in a tree's structure. In fir trees, for example, the patterns at the needle's edge are repeated on branches and then in the shape of the whole tree. Fractal patterns are replicated at many different scales, from the microscopic to the continental.

In natural systems, order and chaos often coexist and interact. The same river which flows smoothly when the bottom is deep and flat, also flows chaotically when the bottom is shallow and covered with rocks.

Many of the concepts in chaos theory don't apply only to the "scientific" world, they are also relevant to the world of individual human beings. Our lives are natural systems exhibiting many of the characteristics of chaos theory.

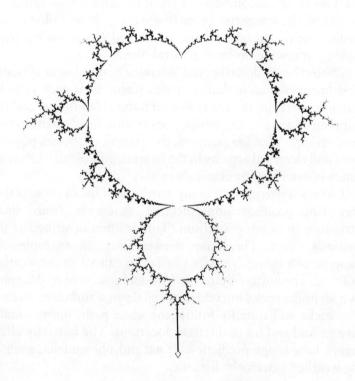

We experience both order and chaos. Predictable outcomes are frequently mixed with unpredictable chaotic outcomes. Small decisions or choices can often have more significant effects than we expect. Fractal-like patterning exists at all levels in our lives – our personal values produce patterns of behavior on hourly, daily and yearly levels.

Thinking about our lives as systems which are both orderly and chaotic provides a powerful mental model for thinking about creative change. It enables us to see transitional (chaotic) periods as times of great opportunity where even small decisions can provide great personal leverage.

This is a very brief introduction to chaos theory. Further implications of chaos theory and its relevance to success and soul will be discussed later in this book.

WHOLE SYSTEMS THINKING

Classical scientific models have generally used deconstructionist and reductionist methods to understand natural phenomena. These approaches have been described as the "child with the watch" method. To understand how the watch works the child breaks it open (deconstruction) and examines each of the pieces separately (reduction). In a somewhat similar vein, physicists use large atom-smashing accelerators to understand the inside of atoms. However, these methods are limited in helping us understand the natural environment and other highly interactive systems.

This has led to recent developments in scientific thinking that have focused on understanding *whole systems*. These developments have been called *systems thinking*. Systems thinking considers patterns and processes. Here the interaction of the individual components is considered to be just as important as the components themselves.

Whole systems approaches are now being applied to a wide range of scientific problems, social phenomena and organizational issues. For example, the interaction of animals, plants, habitat and human activity in the natural environment is best understood by viewing the whole as a system. Similarly, the issue of families in crisis can best be understood by considering the interaction of the many factors in the system – the individuals in the family, the home environment, the wider social context including aspects like the social welfare services involved.

Systems thinking stresses *relationships and connections.* Looking at our lives as whole systems enables us to see, and understand, the roles and effects of relationships and connections. These relationships and connections may include relationships between people, our different work and family commitments, our community and the natural environment.

Systems thinking stresses the *importance of diversity.* Diversity is required for whole systems to function. For example, biodiversity in the environment is often critical to the survival of an individual species. When one important component of the whole system is removed, the entire system can be threatened with extinction.

This principle of diversity has also been applied in the fields of organizational development and competitive market theory. The "systems collapse" in Eastern European government, for instance, has been attributed to some extent to the reduction in diversity promoted by centralized control.

The whole systems focus on *relationships* and *diversity* has implications for individuality, personal success, and soul. These issues, in particular, and their impact at the personal level, will be explored later in this book.

DRAWING FROM EASTERN AND WESTERN CULTURES

It has been said that the most significant discovery of Western culture in the twentieth century has been Eastern culture. Eastern religions, art and philosophy have provided many important insights into the human condition. In many cases, these insights arise from models that contrast directly with our firmly held Western models. Let's look at some of these insights and their relevance to success and soul.

Complexity versus reductionism

In Western cultures, we often define ourselves by simple or one-dimensional labels, for example, "I am a doctor" or "I am creative". We tend to simplify and reduce problems or ideas. Our minds perceive complexity as disorder and anarchy. This reductionist thinking often means subtleties disappear and, with them, meaning and opportunity.

This Western approach is akin to reducing a whole book to a single sentence, for example, "*Hamlet* is the story of a man who could not make up his mind." This does not sound very exciting or interesting. The richness is lost, and we are the worse for it.

In contrast, Eastern cultures tend to retain complexity. They prefer rich diversity. When asked about their personal religion, for example, some Chinese will say that they follow Buddhism, Confucianism and Taoism. They feel no need to define themselves by one religion alone. At the same time, they do not perceive problems, only opportunities, in drawing upon a number of different sources of knowledge.

What can we learn from this about success and soul?

Achieving success certainly requires being able to recognize opportunities. It is also about being flexible and adaptive. Viewing ourselves and the world around us as complex systems increases our ability to be flexible and recognize opportunities.

The soul also thrives on and responds to complexity. An example of this is the way in which great art appeals to us – its depth and layered complexity of meaning touches our soul.

High context versus low context

Western cultures are often described as *low context*, Eastern cultures as *high context*.

One of the companies Stephen used to work with had a number of businesses in Indonesia. The company had a well-developed organizational philosophy and was keen to provide opportunities for all its staff, including the Indonesian staff.

One Indonesian staff member was performing particularly well, working in a team with a number of local colleagues. When a new position became available, the company decided to promote him into it. However, when his Western manager approached him, the engineer said he could not accept the promotion. It would not be "proper" and another colleague should be promoted instead. The manager was puzzled and replied that the colleague was only performing averagely, so why should he get the new position?

The Indonesian man explained that his colleague was from an important, wealthy and respected family. He was older, had been to a good school and was well connected. He therefore felt that his colleague would make a far better choice for the new position even though his work performance had only been fair. As a result the decision was changed and his colleague was given the position. The company believed it was more important to operate in the social context of that country than to impose a context external to it.

This logic appears strange to us. *The main context we consider when evaluating work performance is the work context.* However, in many Eastern cultures, age, family, social status, wealth and relationship contexts are just as important. This is one example of why *Eastern cultures are said to be high context and Western cultures low context.*

Success in Western societies is often defined in a low-context way – focused on a narrow field. It applies to our work or career. It stands apart from the other aspects of our lives.

Conversely, soul is often seen or described as high context – ranging across our entire lives. Soul is concerned with the inner-self, relationships, and the overall environment. Achieving personal success with soul, therefore, is high context – it takes into account everything we do.

The wheel and the ladder

Several years ago we worked in India. It was a fascinating and rewarding experience. During our time there we worked with village people on a rural development project. We learned many of the models that are embedded in Indian culture. One of these models is the *wheel of life*.

Western view of life – the ladder

Eastern view of life – the wheel
(taking the two ends of the ladder
and bringing them together)

In India, people often explain that life is a wheel: we are born, we live, we die and are reincarnated in another life. Life is cyclical – recurrence and transience are two strong themes in this model.

In Western cultures, we tend to view life as a ladder, and the process of living as climbing that ladder. Living is about being born and accumulating things – like power, wealth and objects. It is about progress and advancement, about "moving up in the world", or "climbing the ladder of success". This is a dominant Western model of life.

Eastern cultures understand that energy connects everything in the universe. This energy takes many forms, both material and immaterial; it creates, sustains and destroys. The

Eastern view of life – being born (creating), living (sustaining) and dying (destroying) – is based on the concept of the transformation of energy.

Thinking about our lives in terms of cyclical patterns can help us cope with crises and transitions – they are part of the process of ongoing renewal. The concept of energy and its various forms has considerable relevance to success and soul. Again, these ideas will be discussed in more detail later.

Being versus knowing and doing

We remember the first time we went to India and saw people waiting for trains on railway platforms. A man would sit down near the edge of the platform and – wait. Sitting still, awake and aware of what was going on but doing nothing. We would sit nearby. After a short period of time, we would be bored. Nothing was happening, so we would make something happen. We'd get up and buy a newspaper to read or a few bananas to eat. Meanwhile, the man would continue to sit.

For a short time after, with paper read or food eaten, we would be satisfied. Time would pass, then boredom would set in again. We would look for other things to do. All the time the man would sit patiently, unmoving. What did he know that we didn't? He certainly could wait much better than we could.

Later on, we asked an Indian farmer about this skill of waiting without appearing to do anything. He explained, "Farming is a patient business. When the hot season comes I must wait. Eventually the rains will come, but still I must wait. Only once the ground has softened can I begin the work. After the ground is ploughed and the crop planted I must wait again. Finally, the crops have grown and the harvesting begins. A good farmer is patient – he must learn to wait." He went on. "City people – they always want *to do something* or *to know something*. For farmers, sometimes just *to be* is all that is required. The man who waits on the train station – he is just *being*. When the train arrives then he will go on with the *doing*."

Being is about living in the "now", detaching ourselves from unnecessary activities. To achieve success with real meaning, being is an important dynamic in our lives, along with knowing and doing.

Yin and Yang

In Chinese thought, the Yin and the Yang represent the two poles of nature. They are the symbolic opposites of light and dark, hot and cold, male and female, rational and creative. The Chinese Taoist teachings use the following symbol to represent Yin and Yang.

This symbol has many meanings and interpretations. It symbolizes the continuous cyclic interplay between the opposites. It also illustrates that the seed of one opposite is contained within the major pole of the other opposite.

But what does the Yin and Yang model teach us about our lives? First of all it emphasizes that systems are not balanced; instead, there is a dynamic interaction between opposed states. It also says that natural systems are self-correcting if they are not interfered with. These concepts will be explored in more detail later, when we consider the problems associated with a balanced lifestyle.

Karma, cause and effect

Have you ever noticed that unresolved issues rarely go away? They often seem to wait for us down the road of life. We all put off things we don't like to do. Sometimes we put them off for years, but eventually they seem to catch up with us. Many people describe this as "the law of Karma". Karma, a concept shared by Hindus, Buddhists and many others, means "action". The law of Karma is the law of causality.

> Stephen saw this law in effect several years ago during the period when his grandmother was dying. The family gathered around his grandmother, visiting her at the hospital and helping her to keep her affairs organized. She was frail and weak and, for the first time in her adult life, completely dependent on people around her.
>
> During this time, unresolved family issues kept coming up – issues between mother and child, issues among the children. Some of these relationship and financial issues had lingered unaddressed for years, but it appeared these issues demanded to be raised and resolved before she died.
>
> The family experienced considerable anger and pain during this time. Individual family members argued but eventually worked through these issues, although some of the issues were not resolved until after she died. However, their resolution left people clearer about their relationships with each other, and helped to shape a new family unit after her death.

From talking to people about these events, we know these are common experiences – unresolved issues rarely "go away".

The law of Karma is often stated as "what we do will come back to us". This, however, is oversimplifying things. Karma is not a one-dimensional concept of cause preceding effect, action followed by reaction. It says that all actions are interwoven and interconnected in nature. As a result, we are never isolated from our actions.

Healing is an area where the law of Karma acts. If a person has suffered from a physical trauma, the body sends signals that it is in need of healing. Sometimes that person may choose to ignore these early signals of pain or discomfort. "I'm all right. I'll push through," they say, but if the trauma goes untreated the body will send stronger and stronger signals until the person listens.

This is not to say that the law of Karma is about punishment and reward. It does not say that there is retribution for our actions.

Karma helps us think about building successful habits. For example, rather than always expecting direct rewards for our efforts, Karma teaches us that we need to concentrate on creating positive patterns of action. Rewards may not come immediately, but they may well come later on.

In overview, current wisdom suggests:
- personal success begins from within the individual
- personality has a limited role to play in achieving personal success with real meaning
- the soul exists and is important
- visualizing the future is the first step to creating that future
- we use mental models to conceptualize the world, our behavior and the environment
- seeing our lives as both orderly and chaotic systems is a powerful model for creative change
- focusing on one area of our lives to the exclusion of all other areas will not provide understanding and meaning – we must consider the whole system
- drawing on Eastern and Western models provides opportunities and understanding.

CHAPTER THREE

UNDERSTANDING THE CURRENT DILEMMA

D O YOU EVER FEEL that strong forces are holding you back – preventing you from achieving your goals, maybe even preventing you from clearly defining what those goals might be? Or do you sometimes feel distracted, unable to concentrate on the things you feel you should do, or even unable to define what is worth doing? Why does this happen? What causes these feelings? You may wonder if there are hidden forces at work – unseen dynamics.

The best way out is always through.

Robert Frost

The fact is there *are* hidden forces at work – strong forces, both internal and external. The internal forces include the motivations underlying our personality and habits. People are often told that these internal forces are the only forces at work. "The only thing holding you back is yourself" is typical of what we hear around us, at self-help seminars and personal development workshops. However, real external forces also exist. We all live in a social environment, and that environment influences our actions, attitudes and personal values. People often forget in our affluent consumer society that in countries where drought, poverty or civil war are rife, some people can't "just do it".

To make real change requires us first to be aware of and then to understand the nature of these underlying dynamics. Without that understanding, the change we make will only be superficial and therefore unsustainable. For example, real, sustainable personal change is not simply a matter of understanding our personality or modifying our behavior. These

46

tactical approaches are equivalent to looking at the portion of an iceberg above the water – it only represents a fraction of the total volume. What's happening below the surface is more important. That's where the majority of the iceberg is. Without considering that part, we cannot hope to understand fully what is happening and how to change it.

To advance, any successful strategy must begin with an understanding of the underlying dynamics. What is happening below the surface? What can't we see? Understanding these underlying dynamics will tell us what is really holding us back. It will also provide clues on how we can move forward.

Nelson Mandela discusses this principle in his book *Long Walk to Freedom*. For many years as a political prisoner in South Africa, Nelson Mandela not only survived but managed to strengthen his beliefs. In the hostile prison environment, a key to survival was his understanding of what the authorities were attempting to do – "to break one's spirit and destroy one's resolve". An awareness and understanding of these underlying dynamics enabled Mandela and his fellow prisoners to develop strategies to preserve their human dignity. They realized that they had to fight for prisoners' rights, no matter how small and insignificant. Struggling and gaining these rights symbolized the broader battle against racism and repression in South Africa. Seeing their struggles in this broader context gave meaning to their existence and provided the resolve to survive.

For Nelson Mandela, the combination of a clear personal vision, an understanding of the underlying dynamics, the mutual support of fellow prisoners and a belief in the ability to change the situation ensured his spirit was not broken.

While most of us are unlikely to be in the same situation as Nelson Mandela, these lessons hold true for all of us. Each of us is, in some way, tested by life, and a deep understanding of the external and internal dynamics that act on us is vital. Otherwise we will simply focus on solutions which deal with the most obvious problems or symptoms, instead of developing strategies which tackle the underlying dynamics.

BEVERLEY'S STORY

Doris had worked with Beverley for quite some time. Beverley had spent time working as a secretary before deciding to go back to school and finish a degree. She started her first job after graduating at the age of thirty-two. She was in a hurry to make up for lost time.

The place they worked was tough. The boss worked people long and hard and didn't pay any more than he had to. Beverley was often frustrated and tired. She worked fourteen-hour days on a regular basis, taking work home at night and on the weekend. She worked hard, hoping to get ahead fast. After a year of this, she felt she hadn't got anywhere. The promises of promotion, pay rises and more interesting work were not fulfilled.

Beverley spent a good deal of time complaining to her workmates about how difficult her lot was and how bad the boss was. After a while she seemed like the boy who cried wolf. However, Doris became aware that Beverley was experiencing some new problems. Her partner, Martin, was starting to get sick of the effects of her job. He didn't earn very much either, and her low salary combined with the long hours she always seemed to work made life at home miserable. Beverley was now considering leaving Martin.

At their next regular conversation over coffee, Doris told Beverley of how she had gone through a similar period in her life. What she had realized after a very tough, emotional time that put a lot of strain on her relationship with her partner, was that she needed to shift her focus to the longer term, not just focus on the immediate situation. Doris suggested to Beverley that she seemed to be focusing on the present problems, rather than where she wanted to go.in the longer term and what she wanted out of life. Was it really worth losing Martin over the current job? Was her career that important? And where did she want to be in one year, or in five or ten years' time?

Doris suggested that if Beverley spent a little time, some of it with Martin, thinking through these issues, she would develop a different perspective on the current situation. She might start seeing how irrelevant some of the current concerns were to her long-term goals.

Beverley went home that night and planned some time with Martin to discuss these issues. Soon after their discussion took place, Beverley's mood at work improved significantly. She looked much happier. She began to put in slightly shorter hours and actually ended up with a pay rise!

When they next had coffee together, Doris noted her change of mood. Beverley explained that she now understood how her short-term focus, and her willingness to be a victim of her employer's exploitation, had worked together to cause her personal problems. This was an underlying dynamic in her situation. She had decided that she wanted to spend another six to nine months rounding off her experience in that department and then move on to another part of the company, preferably one with more long-term opportunities.

Beverley's story illustrates the hidden power of the underlying dynamics that shape our experiences, beliefs and actions. The story also illustrates the potential for personal change when we understand these dynamics.

OUR TENDENCY TO FOCUS OUTWARDLY

Humans are well equipped with sensory equipment to hear, see, taste, touch and smell their surroundings. This equipment has been necessary for their survival – hunting and gathering required finely tuned sensory equipment; failure could be injurious or fatal. A focus on the external surroundings ensured a greater chance of survival.

Today there are other reasons why humans focus on the external surroundings. Our fast-paced and exciting world provides a feast of stimulation for all the senses: perfume to smell, different foods to taste, all sorts of music and radio to listen to and a vast array of television and movie images. Most of this external stimulation is not required for our survival or to protect us from danger. Its purpose is to entertain us and gain our attention. However, these images can also be highly influential on our *inner selves*; for example, advertising that promotes products as symbols of success of our consumer society can greatly influence us.

Our ancestors had little control over their incoming stimulation. It got dark and, apart from the light of the fire, it was dark until the sun rose the following morning! Their diets were also less varied and subject to seasonal limitations.

Today, we can choose the incoming stimulation: Want to stay up all night watching TV? Sure, no problem. And those seasonal foods – they are available all year round. Everything is available all the time. This is part of the problem. We often don't know when to stop. Many of us have become stimulation addicts. We reach for excitement and expect it immediately. There are credit cards so we don't have to wait or save, fast food, speedy service, fast travel and rapid communications.

Many parents report that their children will not wait for anything and have short attention spans. Their children expect instant gratification and stimulation. Every year, television programs, movies and video games must be faster, more colorful and louder to capture and maintain children's attention.

What is the impact of all this stimulation? How does it affect us? Often the internal life of the individual suffers. The focus becomes "knowing" or "doing", while "being" suffers. People can be left malnourished and without soul. The soul does not need forty channels of television, action-packed computer games and billboard advertising.

So although humans do tend to focus outwardly, sometimes we need to look inward and nurture our souls. It is like a farmer who does not take care of the land – to keep the land productive it must be rested and nourished. If the farmer does not rest the land, initially it will still produce food, but slowly it will become unproductive. The farmer must feed the land, nourish it and care for it so it will sustain him over time. We must do the same; we must nourish our lives with soul.

WE LET SOMEONE ELSE DEFINE WHAT IS IMPORTANT

Collecting is one way people express their individuality. Bob collects Japanese cartoons on laser disk. He and his friends have hundreds of them. They have built a special viewing room at Bob's house. Bob is not Japanese and you could not even attempt to guess how he became interested in them.

Some people think Bob is a bit strange. He is certainly different. But he does not care much what other people think about his hobby. It's his and that's all there is to it. Bob will talk about it to anyone who is interested and he does not have too much time for those who are not. Bob is unmarried, has a steady, low-key job and limited responsibilities outside his work – what he considers to be a perfect lifestyle for pursuing his hobby.

The degree of individuality shown by people like Bob can seem unusual these days. Real individuality is often labeled as eccentricity. From an early age we are taught to "fit in" and conform. Often we are rewarded for following the social norms and conventions of our friends, work colleagues and families, and ridiculed or abused for our non-observance: "Did you bring the afternoon paper?" is a quip sometimes heard by a work colleague who arrives late to work in the morning.

At the same time, two things we are proud of are our freedom of speech and the ability to express our individuality. Thus, provided we are law-abiding, we are all entitled to express our opinions and to pursue our own personal goals and aspirations. If we wish we can all be individual. Furthermore, we are also told that we should be aware and in touch with what is going on in the world. We are offered opportunities to buy things, participate, express our opinions and be "open" to other points of views.

How often do we exercise that fundamental liberty that we hold so dearly? How often do we let others define what is important to us? How often do we act like followers rather than explorers? And how many of us truly express our own individuality these days?

There are strong forces at work to conform to commonly held values and attitudes. Some of these forces include the media, advertisers and the law. Many times these forces to conform come from the people we consider to be our friends. In today's society, it would be almost impossible to ignore completely all the pervasive messages we receive – to buy this, have that, know this or work towards that.

Often the external messages we receive can have little to do with what is really important to us as individuals. They are part of other people's aspirations or desires, not our own. Finding our own way can be a constant struggle and often it is just easier to conform.

However, without a strong, active sense of our individuality, *discovering and nurturing soul* is difficult. As author Thomas Moore says in his book *Care of the Soul*, "Soul is interested in the differences among cultures and individuals, and within ourselves, it wants to be expressed in uniqueness if not outright eccentricity." According to this premise, it appears that exercising our individuality is integral to achieving a life with soul.

PERSONAL VALUES AND PURPOSE UNCLEAR

Today many of us are out of touch with our personal values and unclear as to our purpose; or we just accept the values and purpose placed on us from outside by others, or the world around us. Sometimes we do this consciously; at other times we are not even aware that we have done so. Often these external values and purpose are presented to us in the form of role models or simplistic stereotypes.

What many of us really need to do now, as individuals, is refocus. *To determine what success means to us we need to clarify our personal values*, the deeply held beliefs or principles that influence our attitudes and actions. Without a very strong sense of who we are and what our personal values are, it is difficult to define and achieve personal success – particularly personal success that is truly meaningful.

Today, with so many messages from the external world telling us what to do and diminishing our individuality, it has become even more difficult. Clarifying our personal values is not easy at the best of times. Therefore we may be more likely to adopt someone else's definition of success.

Personal values such as ambition, the desire for wealth, social recognition and status are commonly espoused in the world around us, for example in movies, the media and advertising. These values underlie the traditional model of success – personal power, money, position and status. While these values have a place in society, they may not reflect who each of us really is as an individual. In contrast, values such as broadmindedness, loyalty and self-discipline, although not as frequently espoused today, may be more important values to us.

Determining our life's purpose should be directly informed by our personal values. However, developing our purpose is difficult without a strong degree of individuality.

Finally, to clarify our values and our purpose it is important to understand the dynamics of which we are a part, and secondly we need effective methods, both of which are currently in short supply. To that end, later chapters of this book provide new insights and tools to do just that – to determine your personal values and life's purpose.

BEHAVIOR NOT ALIGNED WITH PERSONAL VALUES

What drives and determines our actions? Is it our personality, experiences, habits, attitudes, friends or values? All clearly play some role, but how they fit together is not so clear. Sometimes, then, we find ourselves doing things for reasons which are unclear to us. We know it does not sit quite rightly, but we do it anyway. "That's not the real me," we hear people say.

What can be happening is that *our behavior is not aligned with our personal values*. Consider the following questions:
- Do you do things which do not reflect who you really are?
- Do you make commitments which you can't or don't keep?
- Do you say one thing and then do another?
- Do you feel you are in the wrong job?
- Do your friends seem distant and uninterested in what's important to you?
- Do you sometimes experience guilt/anxiety or indecision/vacillation because of your actions?

If some of these questions ring true for you, it may be that your actions and personal values are misaligned. Developing alignment of your personal values, actions and life's purpose is one of the keys to personal success.

THE EFFECTS OF CHANGE ON PEOPLE

"I thought I'd worked out what I wanted to do, but it doesn't seem right now!" This is a common cry of confusion and frustration. It is the student who finishes a course of study and then decides not to pursue that profession. It is the baffled middle manager who questions their career aspirations after being retrenched. It is the people who find themselves lonely and depressed after separation or divorce. Suddenly, yesterday's solutions become today's problems. Why?

We all live in a dynamic system, where an intervention or solution results in *change* in the system. For example, although factories were first built to produce the goods society needed and wanted, they also produced something else – an impact on the environment. As a result, people's views of factories and how they should operate changed. New solutions, such as cleaner production methods, were sought. A solution addresses an issue or situation at the time. However, once the solution is introduced, the system changes, and along with it new problems or issues are created.

Change is a common subject in business.

Stephen once worked closely on a project with the managing director of a large multinational company. During this project they visited an old factory the managing director had managed in England many years previously. He explained how communication between the management and workers had been almost non-existent. When an industrial dispute occurred, it was war.

During one industrial dispute the hostility between the parties led to bricks being thrown through the factory manager's window. The company solution was to lock the workers out of the factory and eventually management defeated the workers in an intense power struggle. It was a bitter dispute, but the management solution was seen as successful at the time.

The managing director of the company explained that now the business world was very different. Direct communication with workers, teamwork and trust were needed to achieve the best solutions. The old way of handling industrial disputes was no longer considered either effective or desirable. He expanded on how this change in thinking had been hard to cope with. All his previously successful solutions were no longer considered effective; they had too many undesirable consequences.

It is the same in our personal lives. New solutions are required as we change and the world around us changes. Solutions we implement must make sense today, not just because they worked yesterday.

LOSS OF MEANING

"The unbearable lightness of being", "the failure of post-modernism" or the "waning of humaneness"; loss of meaning has been variously described. Social workers, teachers and psychologists, among others, are increasingly discussing the problems created by the lack of meaning many people are experiencing in their lives today. Behind many stories of marriage breakdowns, youth suicides, drug and alcohol abuse, and crime are deeply rooted problems relating to loss of personal meaning. Carl Jung said that about one-third of his patients suffered from "senselessness and emptiness" in their lives rather than any specific clinical neurosis.

The widespread loss of meaning is so common today people sometimes assume it has always been like this. That is not so. While loss of meaning has always been part of the human struggle, it has become the plague of the twentieth century. Why has this happened? The reasons are complex and stem from a number of related factors including technological development, rapid population growth, the expansion of cities, the changing nature of work and the breakdown of traditional social support structures.

LOSS OF THE WORD "SOUL"

As has been discussed, soul had become an unfashionable word until very recently. The Christian church revised it out of many religious texts and psychologists became more interested in the mind, in personality and quantitative measurements.

Unfortunately, in urban Western society we now find ourselves experiencing a crisis of loss of meaning. The marginalization of soul as a concept is both symptomatic of, and has contributed to, the current crisis. Neglecting the word "soul" has contributed to the reduction of meaning in people's lives.

However, as has already been discussed, soul is now being talked about again. Talking about soul will help answers emerge. In fact, this book argues that this incorporeal stuff is the missing ingredient for many people in their lives today.

This chapter has explored some of the underlying dynamics that are preventing many of us from moving forward. These underlying dynamics are the part of the iceberg below the surface. They are:

- our tendency to focus outwardly rather than inwardly
- letting someone else define what is important to us and therefore sacrificing our individuality
- not clarifying our personal values and life's purpose
- personal behavior and actions which are not aligned with our personal values
- operating out of a static model of life when it is a dynamic system
- a general loss of meaning
- not paying enough attention to soul.

These dynamics have two major effects: they prevent us from being clear about what we want to achieve and they stop us from achieving our goals once we know what they are. Any effective solution must therefore tackle these underlying dynamics.

In the next chapter, we will examine one of the most commonly proposed solutions to building personal success and soul – a balanced lifestyle.

CHAPTER FOUR

THE PROBLEM
WITH BALANCE

> Most of the change we
> think we see in life
> Is due to truths being
> in and out of favor.
>
> *Robert Frost*

Some years ago, Doris stressed out and was spending most of her waking hours at work. She remembers thinking that if she could balance all the activities she' had to do in her life she would be successful and happy. So she tried to achieve a balance of work, exercise, money, family, sleep and relaxation. She dropped a few unproductive activities and replaced them with those things she had always said she should do, like exercise. She rearranged her schedule and focused on making "quality time" for all these important new activities. Her diary became very full and she was always busy. With considerable effort, she became a pretty good "balancer", even if she does say so herself.

In the short term, balance had some real benefits for Doris. Exercising made her feel much better both physically and mentally. She began to fit in activities she enjoyed that she hadn't allowed herself the luxury to do in the past.

Soon, however, it became obvious that she was not going to achieve very much with this approach if it became the permanent "solution"; least of all personal success with real meaning. Every time she became good at something, or came close to achieving some goal, she would drop it and have to start something else, while an unexpected crisis at work or home would completely upset her balanced lifestyle.

Doris also noticed that she was tending to concentrate a lot on her schedule. Balancing all these activities and competing priorities became an end in itself and the focus of all her various activities.

Worse still, she was putting a lot of energy into trying to balance all these competing priorities and not concentrating on what the activities really achieved. She began to wonder about the benefits of her balanced lifestyle.

It also occurred to Doris that many of the greatest human achievements have nothing to do with balance. Many of the people she admired didn't appear to be too concerned with a balanced lifestyle at all.

What was really going on? A balanced lifestyle sounds like the right solution. It sounds like it should work. But it does not, and worse still, sticking to this belief for so long has led to many of our current problems.

> ...when you reach an equilibrium in biology you're dead...
>
> *Arnold J. Mandell*

There are two main reasons why a balanced lifestyle does not achieve personal success with real meaning. First, *it doesn't directly address the underlying dynamics at work in our lives. It ignores what is really going on. Secondly, it creates new problems that then need to be solved.*

Let's look in detail at some of the reasons why a balanced lifestyle is not the solution to achieving personal success with real meaning.

BALANCE GETS IN THE WAY OF SUCCESS

Most of us could name quite a number of successful people if we were asked to. We know their names and the fields in which they have distinguished themselves – Pablo Picasso in art, Nelson Mandela in politics, Anita Roddick and Jack Welch in business, Mother Teresa in helping the poor and sick, Marie Curie in science and Mozart in music. We usually know specifically what each person's unique achievements have been and the rewards and recognition that have come to them from these achievements.

Sometimes we imagine ourselves in their places. We wish we could achieve this sort of success – the outward trappings of it, anyway. We think much less often about the hard work and hardship that was required to get there.

Balance guarantees a long, safe, healthy life of mediocrity.

Sure, some of these people may be more intelligent than we think we are. But often the key factor leading to their success was single-minded commitment and dedication. It was "perspiration, not just inspiration". Even highly gifted composers like Mozart and Beethoven required over ten years of intensive preparation before they began to produce their greatest works. Nelson Mandela spent many years in jail thinking and planning before he commenced his most productive work. The Nobel Laureate in Economics, Herbert Simon, worked about a hundred hours a week for years before he eventually won the Nobel Prize.

Psychologist John Hayes wrote about the intensive work required to succeed: "In any field, people who want to be creative must expect to invest enormous amounts of time and effort in their profession and even then it may not be enough. The effort involved goes far beyond the hours a normal job requires."

Creation requires an input of energy. The more you want to achieve, the more energy you must put in. That physical and mental energy must come from somewhere and it must be focused. Contrast this to a balanced lifestyle, where energy is spread around thinly – a little here and a little there.

Now, think of a time when you had a special job to do – an important project of some kind. It may have been anything – planning a wedding, preparing for a big presentation at work.

These projects don't just "fit in" with the run-of-the-mill things in your life. You have to put in a great deal of time and energy. This time and energy must come from somewhere, so you re-prioritize, spend less time exercising or doing your hobbies or, maybe, sleeping.

Sometimes you find reserves of energy you didn't know you had. Even though you didn't think you could stay up until 3 a.m. preparing a report or looking after a sick friend, you do it. It is important enough for you to give a lot of yourself.

Most people will willingly lose sleep when it comes to having a baby. They realize that it is worth putting other things on hold while they get involved with this important task. Their sleep suffers, and as a result they sometimes perform less well in other areas of their lives. But for that time, it doesn't matter to them – it is worth it. A balanced lifestyle simply does not support this "drop everything" kind of commitment.

> Just because you *can* juggle a large number of competing priorities does not always mean it is a good idea to do it.

> Substantial achievements not only take extra energy, they often involve destroying something. An image that Doris saw recently in a television documentary about professional dancers comes to mind. It opened with a beautiful and famous ballerina gliding across the stage, perfect and graceful. However, after the performance when she removed those sweet little shoes there were two tightly bound feet inside. She unbound them and her feet were bruised, deformed and bleeding. The ballerina revealed that she experienced constant pain throughout her practice and performance.

Damaging oneself is in direct opposition to the idea of balance. Inflicting pain and suffering to achieve something is anything but balanced, and although it is not always necessary to suffer to these extremes, it is important to realize that a balanced lifestyle may compete with the achievement of success.

Success also requires creative change. Creative change requires us to shift out of our comfort zone, to think and act in new ways. Balance gets in the way of success because it stifles creativity and obstructs change.

Young people know this. They usually don't seek balance in their lives. In fact, they often rebel against it. They know that it stifles their creativity. They are young enough to hear their intuition tell them that balance is not the answer. It is later in life, as adults, when we settle down, take on too much and begin to feel the effects of our lifestyle that we start to think of a balanced lifestyle as the solution.

Many creative people do work to a regular routine. This, however, should not be confused with a balanced lifestyle. This is discipline, and discipline and commitment are important allies for people who want to be creative and successful.

In summary, among the fundamental principles of success and human action are:

• To achieve success we must concentrate energy, and usually not just once, but over and over again.
• Achieving success usually involves forgoing less important activities.
• Achieving success can have both destructive and creative outcomes.

Where does a balanced lifestyle fit in with all this talk about success? The truth is that it doesn't. In fact, a balanced lifestyle often works against success, unless you define success in your life as achieving a balanced lifestyle. This leads us to the next problem with balance.

FOCUSING ON BALANCE DOES NOT GIVE MEANING

"What am I trying to achieve? I am trying to achieve a balanced lifestyle." We hear these kinds of commitments a lot, but *defining success in terms of a balanced lifestyle does not provide meaning*.

It's like saying, for example, you want to achieve "good health". Certainly, your health is worth working on – all of us do need to sustain ourselves. However, a key benefit of good health is that it allows us to do things we want to do. Good health *enables* us to pursue what is important to us.

Likewise, a focus on balance does not provide us with meaning in our lives. Emphasis placed on pursuing balance for meaning is hollow. It often detracts from the more important task of working on our life's purpose. Imagine your epitaph:

Think about when you are most satisfied with your life. Is it when your life is most balanced, or when you are creating something and your life is less balanced?

Two fundamental tenets of this book are that we have to become aware of our own values and attitudes, and that we then need to use this awareness as a catalyst for creative change. This creative change will then help lead us towards our life's purpose and to personal success with real meaning. A balanced lifestyle does not address these fundamental issues.

First, balance does not operate within solidly based personal values. It tends to place more or less equivalent value on a wide range of activities. In this way, a balanced lifestyle does not help us align our actions with our personal values.

Secondly, the pursuit of a balanced lifestyle is often externally driven. After all, who determines *what* needs to be balanced – ourselves, our friends or the media? How many new activities do we try to squeeze into our busy schedules because someone else says it is important? "You must do this", "You should see that" – people such as our friends, work colleagues and the media can all be very persuasive.

> Uncluttering our lives, and disengaging ourselves from activities which are not about who we really are, is a key to personal success.

Finally, balance is about achieving a *condition* rather than long-term goals. Focusing on a balanced lifestyle frequently becomes a simple time-management issue. We spend more time thinking about what we should be doing on a week-to-week basis, rather than spending quality time thinking about long-term issues. A balanced lifestyle places the focus on urgent tactical concerns, rather than on important strategic issues.

Once you have clarified your values and begin to operate in alignment with these, balance will cease to be an issue in your life. You will focus on what is truly important to you. You will no longer feel the need to balance a range of activities, some or all of which may be intrinsically unimportant to you.

HOW DO YOU ALLOCATE TIME FOR SOUL?

In the balanced lifestyle model, time is allocated to a range of activities. How, then, does soul fit in? How do you allocate time for soul? Do we try to "balance" those activities that have no soul with those that have soul? This approach is fundamentally flawed. Soul is not simply a time-management issue. Soul does not need an exercise routine, nor to be squeezed into our busy schedule. However, this is what many people striving for balance often do. They accept that much of what they do – their work, for instance – has no fundamental meaning for them. In their "balanced" lifestyle they then attempt to schedule in one or more activities that are meaningful to them.

While we are not always free to decide how we spend our time, and certain necessary activities may actually be "soulless", we do need to be nourished with soul. There are times when we need more of this nourishment than at others, particularly when our lives may feel empty and hollow. The balance model suggests that a regular "dose" of soul will keep us going. This is usually not enough. What we really need is the rich interweaving of soul throughout the whole fabric of our lives.

BALANCE DOES NOT ACKNOWLEDGE THE DYNAMIC SYSTEM MODEL

Biology tells us that life can be considered as a series of dynamic systems. For example, as water levels diminish in an area, animal species must respond. Those species which can survive on less water stay and may increase in numbers. Those species which cannot survive on the reduced water supply either move away or die. Whole systems are constantly adjusting to changes in their environment. In this way, living systems are in a perpetual state of flux. Change is a constant feature of natural systems.

In fact, biological systems become "nervous" when things become too stable. They generate their own "destabilizing" energy in these situations. Consider the response of the human brain when a person is placed in an environment with no external stimulation, for example an isolation tank. After a short period of time, the brain begins to generate its own images – often richly colorful and fantastic. Biological systems appear to "know" that "stability is death". As a consequence, they become nervous when things become too stable. So when some people pursue balance or stability they often seem only to achieve a sense of meaninglessness. From a biological systems perspective, this is not surprising.

Barbara lived in a beautiful new house in a nice leafy suburb. She and her husband Allen had it built for them a couple of years ago. It was something they both had strived for and they were very excited about it when they moved in. Both Barbara and Allen had successful careers in large international corporations. They put in long hours at their jobs, but most evenings they found some time to relax in front of the TV. They prided themselves on keeping fit and healthy and maintaining balanced diets. On weekends they entertained at home and both actively pursued interesting hobbies.

They earned large salaries which they enjoyed spending on modern furniture, vacations to exotic locations and eating out at expensive restaurants. They wore designer clothes and had fashionable friends. They seemed to be the perfect couple and with their new house, their life seemed to have reached perfection itself. They were relatively affluent and their lives could also be described as "well balanced".

Not long after moving into the house, Barbara began to feel something was wrong with her life. She felt the problem was her husband. Allen was happy with the house, his job and his hobbies. But he didn't want to do or try anything new. Barbara felt Allen was settling down and she was starting to feel restless. He wasn't really very interested in dinner parties, so she stopped having people over to dinner. This was the life she thought she had always wanted, but now she felt stifled. She wanted some fun and excitement.

Despite some months of counselling, Barbara and Allen decided to separate and divorce. Allen moved out and later the house was sold. Both were disappointed, but accepted that this was the best thing. Barbara started seeing old girlfriends and began to enjoy life again.

Barbara's story is a common one and can be interpreted in a number of different ways. One of them is that balance was part of the problem. A close friend who had became aware of the problems had urged Barbara to drop everything and focus on fixing the relationship with her husband. She didn't, and Allen didn't either. Instead of taking weeks off work, spending sleepless nights in stressful, tearful arguments and dealing with the central, problematic issues, they maintained their normal routines. Their jobs had to be done and so forth. The desire for balance did not allow the space and energy for dealing with this issue.

Much of what we are told today involves the idea that balance is the answer to our hectic lifestyles. However, we are "biological systems" and even those of us who prefer security and conformity will often feel the "pull" that comes from doing too well at achieving a balanced lifestyle.

Like Barbara and Allen's experience, balance pursued in place of purpose can paradoxically lead to major personal upheavals. This book is about the transition from a balanced life to a meaningful life.

It is time to initiate a shift in our understanding. We need to move on. The sooner we realize that the answer does not lie in a balanced lifestyle, the sooner we can develop workable solutions to some of our problems. By understanding what our personal values are and being more in touch with who we are, we can begin to create a purposeful and enjoyable life, not just one that is balanced for its own sake.

In the next chapter, we will commence this process by looking at how we can think differently about personal success and soul.

CHAPTER FIVE

INTEGRATING SUCCESS
WITH SOUL

H AVING LOOKED at some of the problems with trying to integrate success and soul, let us go back to basics and reclaim some old wisdom.

We can't talk about achieving success with soul without talking about meaning – that meaning which provides our own unique and personal answer to life. Looking at the issue of the meaning of life establishes the framework for refining our conceptions of success and soul.

> Everything should be
> made as simple as
> possible, but not simpler.
>
> *Albert Einstein*

Unfortunately nowadays, talking about the meaning of life tends to be considered unfashionable or pretentious. As soon as "the meaning of life" is mentioned, people roll their eyes skyward or look at you like you're from Mars.

And yet, isn't it a most important question? Certainly, for many of us grappling with this strange world we live in, whether we articulate it or not, it is very important. "What's the point?" We hear this said regularly. It is just another way of saying, "Where's the meaning in it?"

There are many pressures on people today, like high unemployment and the contradictory messages we receive from the world. People's disillusionment is reflected in outcomes such as high crime rates, widespread substance abuse and increasing suicide rates. People are looking for answers and meaning.

In this chapter, we are going to look at meaning in a new way. As film star Mae West aptly quipped, "It's not the men in my life that counts – it's the life in my men." Mae had a habit of putting things in a new way. If we use the same kind of logic, perhaps we can say, "It's not the meaning *of life* that counts, it's the meaning *in your life.*"

THE TWO TYPES OF MEANING

There are two fundamental parts to the "meaning of life" question – the general and the specific. The general part of the question is, "Why does life exist at all?" or "Why are we *all* here?" The specific part of the question is, "What is *my* purpose or part within it?" or "Why am *I* here?"

To understand the difference between the two parts of the question, it helps to think about life as a movie. A movie is *about* something; it sets out to do something; it has a reason for being. An example might be a movie which sets out to show life in country England in the 1800s. That's the general part of the question: "Why is the movie made?"

And then I have a role to play in it. My role fits within the context of the big picture (literally!) and contributes to the overall reason for the picture. This is the specific part of the question: "What is my part in the movie about?" I am setting out to play a character to the best of my ability, and my character has something to say and do that contributes to the movie. In the example above, my role might be to portray a farmer of that era.

These two parts can be put down as two sentences that need to be completed:
• The meaning of life is…
• My purpose or role in life is…

We can start with the first part of the question (the general), then use our answer to shed light on the second part of the question (the specific). Alternatively, we can consider the second part of the question

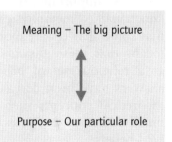

Meaning – The big picture

Purpose – Our particular role

(my role), and this may help shed light on what the broader, more general, meaning of life is.

In the past, many thinkers spent a lot of time considering the meaning of life. While no one view will be promoted here, their ideas certainly provide us with some food for thought.

Considering some of their answers may help us clarify these answers for ourselves. If you have not previously considered these questions, you may see answers which make sense to you. Many people find they are unconsciously operating out of one of these views already.

As we look at these answers, it is important to remain clear about which of the two questions is being answered – the general or the specific. For example, consider a religious answer: "The meaning of life is to serve God." This is a general answer; for many people it answers the question, "Why does life exist at all?" Within this, someone's specific purpose as an individual may be to heal the sick. This, then, would be that person's specific way to serve God; it answers the question, "Why am I here?"

SOME THOUGHTS ON THE MEANING OF LIFE

English philosopher Keith Britton summarizes the philosophical answers to the meaning of life into three categories: doctrinal, metaphysical and informal.

It is important to note, however, that the terms "doctrinal", "metaphysical" and "informal" do not imply that some answers are more correct than others. "Doctrinal" means that these answers have arisen from doctrines such as a religious set of beliefs or principles. "Metaphysical" answers have been derived from the philosophical study of theoretical concepts such as *being*, *identity* and *the mind*. Finally, *informal* indicates answers that constitute commonly held beliefs.

Doctrinal answers

There are generally considered to be three doctrinal answers to the meaning of life. They are all based around God and our role in God's plan.

One view which might be called "our role in the great master plan" is that God has a master plan for the whole world. This plan for the whole world can only be achieved if each person finds and completes that part of the plan to which God has assigned them. This answer addresses both the general and the specific questions. It implies that life is like a large jigsaw puzzle in which our life forms one of the pieces.

The second view might be called "our role as sinners", and is based upon the notion of God's glory and our depravity or weakness. Therefore, the world, as we know it, exists as an expression of God's glory: men and women are included because, being sinful, they need redemption and redemption is the supreme expression of God's glory. Again, both the general and the specific questions are answered.

The third view could be described as "our role in the dress rehearsal". This is a much less definite answer, stating that we exist in the world in order to prepare ourselves for another life – a life after death. This might suggest that our focus should be directed to the "hereafter" rather than our existence in this mortal life. This view answers the specific question, "Why am I here?" It also implies that this world was created to prepare us for the next. This would then answer the general question, "Why are we all here?"

All doctrinal answers have a number of things in common. They all presuppose the existence of an after-life and the existence of God.

A metaphysical answer

Aristotle, one of the great Greek philosophers, spent a lot of time on the issue of the meaning of life along with many other "big" issues. His view represents a rather prevalent one amongst Greek philosophers of the time. The Aristotelian answer holds that the meaning of life lies in the *pursuit of knowledge*.

It does seem a little ironic that a group of people who spent most of their lives pursuing knowledge might then think that the meaning of life was the pursuit of knowledge. This answer surely would have comforted Aristotle and his fellow thinkers. Many academics today may well agree that the meaning of life for human beings is to pursue knowledge. Similarly, it might not be surprising that the church might think that the meaning of life revolves around God.

Some informal answers

A range of informal answers to the meaning of life question are prevalent today and describe what the meaning of life is for some people. Again, to describe them as informal is not to diminish their validity. They are simply what some people may describe as the general meaning of life or, more often than not, what the specific meaning is in their own individual lives.

For some people it is *work* that provides meaning in their lives. It certainly seems that work is an important ingredient of a meaningful existence. The famous psychologist Sigmund Freud, among his less controversial statements, said that love and work form the basis of a happy life.

For other people, the meaning of life is *loyalty to an institution or community*. For example, "I am here to serve my country, my church, my university, my school."

One of the most prevalent "institutions" which provides meaning to people's lives is *the family*. Many people who work, have hobbies and pursue all kinds of other activities, would state that the one thing that provides them with meaning is their family. The rest of life is just spent passing time or doing what must be done in order to support their family.

A whole range of activities that provides meaning in people's lives revolves around *helping others*. We all know people who see their primary roles as serving other people. They may fulfill that role in a range of settings – home, their job, volunteer work, etc. This meaning is often described by phrases such as "we are here to serve others"; "to do what good we can"; or, "to leave the world a better place than we found it". This is a popular view held by modern ethicists.

Another rather popular view is that "I am here *to realize my own nature to the full* or *to be myself as fully as I can*". This is a commonly held view among sportsplayers and people interested in personal growth. Many people who follow this view define personal success in terms of personal fulfillment and excellence. While this view may lead to self-centered actions, it does not need to. Many great leaders have espoused and operated from this meaning.

Another important view that should be added to this list is that espoused by Victor Frankl, a psychologist who is famous for his writings on the meaning of life. Frankl says that the meaning of life is *to retain our dignity and our basic human goodness despite what life serves out to us*. Again, it is important to look at what may have led Frankl to this view. Frankl formulated his views through his experiences in a Nazi concentration camp. Victor Frankl observed that many of those best able to cope and survive had a strong sense of their life's purpose. That sense of meaning fostered a will to live and act with dignity despite the appalling conditions.

Finally, *social movements* can provide meaning in people's lives. Recently, many people have felt greater responsibility for the sustainability of the planet. For some people this has become their "calling". Whether it is the protection of species and natural habitat, or reduction in "greenhouse" emissions, the underlying meaning is found in actively caring for the environment.

Two people, two meanings

Another important aspect of meaning is that two different people may ostensibly be doing the same thing – in psychological terms, their actions may be the same – but the two people will place different meanings on their actions. This is best illustrated by a story set in the Middle Ages.

> A man walks up to a field where a huge cathedral is being built. A number of stonemasons are working on the building. Each mason is using a hammer and chisel to carve a piece of stone. The man asks each of the masons the same question: "What are you doing?"
> "I'm chipping this stone," says the first.
> "I'm building a wall," says the second.
> "I'm becoming a skilled tradesman," says another.
> "I'm supporting my family," says another.
> "I'm building a church," says another.
> "I'm worshiping God," says another.

What the stonemasons are outwardly doing and what is happening internally are quite different things. In other words, the same actions may be motivated by totally different meanings. We have to ask what the meaning of that action is for that individual. This is critical to our understanding of meaning in life.

As has been discussed in this chapter, there are many different views about the meaning of life. These are based on our perceptions and interpretations. There is no definitive answer. What is meaningful to one person may not provide meaning for someone else.

Furthermore, it is our own personal answer to the "meaning of life" which needs to underlie our definition of success. In other words, inherent in each meaning is a picture of what success would be. When we define what life means to us, we are also stating what success means. For example, if I define meaning in my life through my work, then I believe that success must come from my efforts at work. Alternatively, if I define meaning in terms of "my role in God's master plan", then for me success is found in fulfilling that role.

Soul is also about meaning, particularly inner meaning. This explains the sense of inner meaninglessness we feel when we do things that don't provide us with soul. In this way, *our search for meaning is the search for success with soul.*

And what is the consistent theme in *all* these different views on the meaning of life? If we look closely at each of them, what we find is that they do all come down to one fundamental. That fundamental is *relationships*. Relationships are the consistent theme. The relationship with ourselves (concerning personal fulfillment, knowledge or human dignity), with other people around us (concerning family, community, institutions or the helping of others), with God (concerning personal religion or faith), with our vocation (concerning work), and with our surroundings (concerning the environment).

Soul is also about relationships – the relationship of ourselves with God, with others, or with a "cosmic soul" such as the environment. Relationships are the common threads that link meaning, success and soul.

And, it is the quality of these relationships that is important. Many of the central conflicts in the world stem from relationship problems. Wars between countries, family breakdowns, divorces, damage to the environment, even our own internal conflicts, are all examples of relationship conflicts. Much unhappiness and dissatisfaction in life is a result of poor relationships. A great deal of the "hollow" success that exists is success without quality relationships. *To achieve success with soul, we must find ways to improve the quality of our relationships.*

In fact, we believe that we should go further, and that success needs to be redefined in terms of relationships. In this way, we can shift the emphasis of success solely from ourselves to ourselves *and* others *and* the environment. Put simply, we believe success should be defined as follows:

Success is achieving quality relationships with ourselves, with others and with the environment.

We call this new definition of success the *relationship model* of success. This is the model of success we need to achieve success with soul.

This new definition of success and how we can achieve it will be discussed in the remaining chapters. In the next chapter, we will expand on this new model of success and identify the key relationships it encapsulates. We will also define what "quality" relationships are and describe actions that can help us build them.

CHAPTER SIX

THE RELATIONSHIP MODEL
OF SUCCESS

A comprehensive view reveals no such thing as personal self-actualization apart from the self's role or the self's niche in the larger ecosystem of civilization and the biosphere. The vision of an independent self to be fulfilled is a lethal mirage.

Ralph Wendell Burhoe

THE PRECEDING CHAPTER introduced a new way of looking at success – a way incorporating soul. This view says success is created through quality relationships with ourselves, with others and with the environment. We have called this new model of success "the relationship model of success".

This model emerges from systems thinking, which considers not only the individual components of a system, but also what occurs between them – the energies or relationships.

The relationship model of success considers all the key components of the system we live in *and* all the connections between those components. As a result, the relationship model of success places the individual's success in a larger context.

We can build on this new model of success by identifying some of the key relationships in the model and the activities which help build those quality relationships.

THE INDIVIDUAL

Let's begin with the individual. The relationship model of success says that personal success begins with creating quality relationships between the mind, the body and the soul.

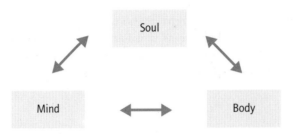

Mind, body and soul have been the focus of considerable discussion and literature throughout human history. One of the most hotly debated issues is to what extent they exist as separate entities. Some have argued that the distinction between body and mind is antiquated. Certainly modern medical research has highlighted some of the physical factors underlying mental illness and, in so doing, has provided evidence for one type of link between the body and the mind.

These issues are not going to be discussed in detail here. We don't need to delve into these distinctions to begin to make a difference to our lives. In fact, "paralysis by analysis" can set in, with intellectualism becoming the objective, rather than positive change. We can simply acknowledge that there are different views relating to mind, body and soul. These views do not negate the argument that personal success begins with creating quality relationships between mind, body and soul.

> This is a world of process, not a world of things.
>
> *Margaret J. Wheatley*

What does this really mean? How do we do this? Building quality relationships starts with being aware that mind, body and soul are all part of us. Some people deny the "soul" of their being and in doing so miss out on a vital element in achieving meaningful success.

However, even when people accept the existence of all three elements – mind, body *and* soul – they often consider it

83

in an academic way and it does not translate into change in their own lives. They might argue theoretically that the soul "exists", but then behave as if it is not part of their own self. So let's now look more closely at how awareness of these elements of ourselves can translate into meaningful change.

The processes which operate at the individual level can be conceptualized as *knowing, being* and *doing.* Knowing involves our thinking processes – our perceptions, emotions, memories and our rational thoughts. Being is about our sense of self, our soul and our individuality. Doing relates to our actions, which are in turn influenced by mental elements – our values, attitudes, motivation, commitment, personality and previous experiences.

If we accept that the mind, body and soul form the key elements of our self, then meaningful change is change that affects our knowing, being and doing.

This leads us to the next point: not only do each of these elements – the mind, the body and the soul – need to be cared for, but our actions need to support the whole system. When our actions are in alignment with our values – when we positively exercise our conscience, and when we reflect on our actions – we grow as individuals. In this way, we strengthen the internal processes which support us and enhance the experience of "wholeness". We see this in someone who "walks the talk", someone whose actions are in alignment with their beliefs and values.

THE SOCIAL

John Donne, the famous sixteenth-century poet, said that "no man is an Island, entire of it self". It is true. We live in a world inhabited by other people. We interact with other people at home, at work, in our community and in our circle of friends and acquaintances. As individuals, we are embedded in a social system.

We interact with the people around us in many different ways and on many different levels. At the most fundamental level we share the space in which we live. In this physical space we can be very close to others, sometimes touching, at other times very far away from them. In fact, we often communicate with each other in physical ways. Communication can have cognitive components, such as sharing our thoughts, and emotional components, for example how we feel. We can also interact at a spiritual level. Almost all significant relationships have some form of "soul-to-soul" interaction.

The quality of these social relationships is a key to achieving success with soul. *The relationship model of success says there is no such thing as personal success without other people's success.* "Not very earth-shattering," we hear you say. "Don't we already know this?"

Certainly, we often hear people accepting awards who thank "all the people without whose help this would not have been possible..." This "support crew" model is not what the relationship model is all about. It's not about thanking all the people who helped one person become successful. This is the old model of success.

The relationship model of success says, "This award is the result of the efforts of a group of successful people." It belongs to all of them.

Successful person

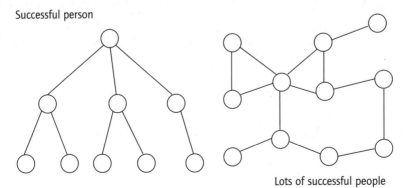

Lots of successful people

The relationship model of success is non-competitive. It says we are interdependent. Building relationships with others is more important than beating them at something. People who operate out of the relationship model, even when they are in a competitive situation, only see this as an opportunity to push themselves to achieve their own personal best. They don't see their own achievements in terms of reducing the self-worth of others. They enjoy the friendship of their fellow competitors, with whom they share a common interest.

This model of success also helps us understand success in a team. In their book *The Wisdom of Teams*, authors Jon Katzenbach and Douglas Smith indicated that high-performance teams have members "committed to one another's personal growth and success". Successful teams not only get the job done, they care about relationships. In this context, team building can be seen as improving the quality of the relationships in the team.

The so-called "win/win" frame of mind is only possible when we operate out of the relationship model of success. Success built on relationships is not selfish or self-centered. It is not about personal fulfillment to the exclusion of others. When we operate out of the relationship model of success we search for mutually beneficial solutions.

Contribution to others lies at the heart of meaningful success.

Activities which can build quality relationships in our social environment include spending time with family, taking time to listen and support colleagues at work, and active community contribution and involvement.

Relationships and relationship-building activities create "positive energy". This positive energy helps us to grow, helps others to grow and can contribute both to our own success and to the success of others. It's like the old saying: "What goes around, comes around." *The positive energy we create in our relationships comes back to us in the form of success with soul.*

THE ENVIRONMENT

It has often been said that with freedom must come responsibility. Never has this adage been more true than currently, with respect to the environment. Our ability to affect our natural environment has increased enormously, but our sense of responsibility toward it is only just starting to develop.

The term environment refers to the specific surroundings in which we find ourselves. At one level this is the planet; more immediately it is our homes, our places of work and our local surroundings. These all constitute environmental systems of which we are a part.

A variety of processes occurs at the environmental level. In our homes we use water, energy, air and space. We consume materials and dispose of waste. At work, there may be a larger system which could include anything from the office air-conditioning to a factory processing materials. Beyond our homes and work is the greater environment. There are also natural ecosystems and nature's own manufacturing and recycling processes.

> If we don't support the system that supports us – we die.
>
> *Rod Harris*

> Ignore it and it will go away...
>
> *Unknown*

Activities which forge a quality relationship with the environment include increasing our awareness of environmental issues, reducing our energy usage and active participation in environmental programs. To achieve success which cares for the environment, these activities need to occur at all levels: at home, at work and on a global level. Otherwise, we just "throw the trash into our neighbor's yard".

It is still not clear what the full implications of our responsibility as caretakers of the environment will be. However, it is important to stay informed as our global understanding develops. Our relationship with the environment will not go away; we are, after all, dependent on it.

Sympathetic environmental settings can also provide soul. When our houses are filled with things of personal meaning, expressing who we are – soul is found. At work, well-designed meeting places and sensitivity to office layout can improve our work experience. Natural environments can provide soul through our interactions with them.

THE INDIVIDUAL, SOCIAL AND ENVIRONMENTAL

When we place all of the individual, social and environmental relationships together we have a system, expanding out from us into our social settings, then out into the environment. An expanding universe of connections from our individual selves, this system is a richly woven fabric of interdependencies.

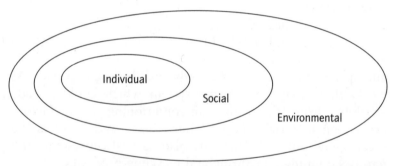

This system is not in "balance", or equilibrium, and does not survive by seeking stability. It is a dynamic system at all levels. Change, renewal and transformation are its characteristic elements. Diversity and complexity are vital for its existence. Processes which maintain and develop individual elements and strengthen their connections ensure that the whole system grows.

Processes which reduce complexity and diversity cause the system to wither. We observe this phenomenon in the natural environment and it is also true of our social interactions. Where the desire, belief and commitment are present, our interpersonal relationships tend to grow, becoming richer and more complex. Conversely, without these essential ingredients, our relationships with others tend to wither, becoming stale in repetitive one-dimensional patterns. Significant partnerships like marriages often display this tendency, either strengthening or spiraling downward into decay.

When we look at all these connections, the idea of personal control is illusory. How can we possibly control this complex system? All we can do is act purposefully within the system, intent on improving the quality of the relationships we have.

This system forms the framework in which we operate. We put "flesh on the bones" by providing content from our own lives. We invest our energy in areas which strengthen and build relationships which are important to us.

When you operate out of the relationship model of success you will live a responsible and meaningful life. You will also find that as you change yourself, the world around you will change. As you become more focused, people respond to you differently. When you are clear about who you are and where you are going, you display personal leadership. Other people who share your vision will follow. Those going in other directions will drift away.

So, how does it all fit together? What does success with soul look like?

The fact is that it can look like a lot of things. It looks like a senior executive or president in a multinational corporation. It looks like a mother at home with her new baby. It looks like a person running their own small business. It looks like a young guy working part-time who spends most of his time doing what he really loves – skateboarding.

We'd like to take some time to tell just a few stories of success. These are stories about exceptional people who are not doing things that society may necessarily call successful by its usual standards, but people who are operating out of the relationship model of success.

Mandy is a good friend of ours and we are privileged to know her. She has spent over ten years as a music therapist working with profoundly mentally handicapped children. These are children who can't even do the most basic things we all take for granted. Most cannot walk, talk or feed themselves. Some show no sign of comprehension or understanding at all.

We once asked Mandy about her work. She said, "You don't get much feedback most of the time. I get the kids everyone else hasn't been able to do anything with. I try to reach them with music; flutes, drums, all sorts of stuff. Mainly, I don't get much reaction. But every now and then, maybe only every few weeks or so, I'll see a spark, just a small spark – and that's success. That keeps me going for a long time. That makes it worth it."

Anita Roddick, founder and managing director of The Body Shop, would be considered a success by many people's standards because she heads a multinational corporation which makes millions of dollars a year.

Anita would probably also consider herself a success. However, her reasons would be more likely to revolve around the fact that she has created a business in line with her strong personal values and business ethics. It is a business which puts back into the community and the environment, rather than just taking out, and one that has also acted as a demonstration to other business leaders that a business can have both success *and* soul.

Several years ago we visited an Aboriginal community in northern Australia. During the day we went out into the Australian outback with a number of the Aboriginal people. They showed us the native foods they eat and the traditional medicines they still use. They described how they lived off the land and told stories from the Dreamtime. Back at the community they taught us traditional arts such as bark painting and how to make music playing a traditional instrument, the didgeridoo. Throughout the day they told us the story of their community.

Some years ago the local elders decided they needed to make some changes to their community. They wanted to ensure that their young people retained their cultural heritage and sense of identity. They also realized that people in the community needed jobs and meaningful work. The community leaders decided to start a number of businesses. These included having tourists visit the community and learn about their culture. This would help keep their culture alive as well as creating understanding.

Five years later the community has won a number of prestigious tourism awards and many tourists from all over the globe visit them each week. The community is strong and although their business does not earn them a large amount of money, it has given them something they all work on together. The people are proud of what they have built and have a five-year plan for taking the business into the future. When we heard the Aboriginal people speak about their community and the business they had created – founded on their principles and values – we could hear in their voices and see in their faces that this community was a group of successful people.

All these people measure their success by their own criteria and they remind us that success can look like many different things. Even more importantly, perhaps, these stories tell us that success is more than just what we see.

CHAPTER SEVEN

BEYOND BALANCE:
DYNAMIC TENSIONS

The stillness in stillness is not the real stillness. Only when there is stillness in movement can the spiritual rhythm appear which pervades heaven and earth.

Taoist saying

Training people can be a rewarding but at times frustrating experience. Stephen used to work training young professionals to operate complex computer software. It took days to train someone adequately and to ensure that they would be up to speed by the end of the course. Sometimes course participants would type the wrong keys and make the same mistakes over and over again.

To make matters worse, the training was often "on the job". Management wanted their employees to learn the new software as they continued to do their work. It was very frustrating, seeing people with urgent work to complete, trying to do so on software they had yet to master. Sometimes Stephen felt the urge to take over the keyboard and do the job himself. That way some of the work would get done in time.

Parents can have a similar experience with their children. They know they need to teach their children and let them learn at their own pace, but as their patience wears thin, they often take over and finish the job themselves. Think of the times when children want to help prepare a meal or want to get themselves dressed and ready to go out the door.

In both of these situations there is a tension between the need to get the job done and the need for learning. A short-term need competes with a longer-term requirement and frustration comes from the *tension between the two competing priorities*.

We often have competing priorities in our lives: between work and family, exercise and relaxation, doing our own work or helping others with theirs. *Managing these competing priorities is one of the keys to personal success.*

When we talk about managing, however, we are not talking about time-management. Most time-management approaches focus on just one thing – time. They have us making lists, running diaries and squeezing more out of our days and weeks. These time-management approaches can end up creating more priorities rather than less, adding new activities and responsibilities rather than removing those that provide little meaning.

Moreover, many time-management approaches are too tactical to solve problems of competing priorities. Why? Because these approaches operate out of the old "balanced lifestyle" model, a model which has us thinking mainly about how much time we spend in each activity. Although they are sometimes useful, these one-dimensional approaches rarely lead to the sort of deep questioning that is required to find innovative long-term solutions.

Dynamic systems in tension

Systems thinking is a much better, more creative approach to considering competing priorities in our lives. *Systems thinking recognizes that competing priorities exist in "dynamic tension".* What is dynamic tension?

Dynamic tension is easy to understand. Pick up an elastic band. Hold it out in front of you between both hands. Pull it apart until it is tight. This system is now in tension.

Now hold one hand still and pull the other hand further away. See how the amount of tension in the system increases? The system responds dynamically. It pulls back, trying to keep the elastic band in the same place.

Next, move both hands further apart at the same time and see how much more force is required. Again, the whole system is dynamic; it responds to the forces that act upon it.

Put simply then, *a system in dynamic tension contains the objects and the forces or energies which link the objects.* When we are talking about dynamic tension in our lives, the "objects" may be activities, issues, priorities or events.

A system in dynamic tension is characterized by *action, change* and *reaction.* Conversely, the popular but limited "balance model" is like an old-fashioned set of scales. When more weight is added to one side, the other side moves up. To balance the scales we have to put more weight on one side or take some weight off the other.

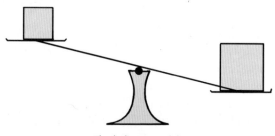

The balance model

The balance model reminds us that our time is finite. We only have so much to "spread around". However, the only solution provided is to balance the two sides of the scales by equalizing the two weights; in other words, by dividing our time or energy equally between two areas of our lives.

By comparison, the *dynamic tension model* – the elastic band between two hands – focuses our attention on *the forces acting between the two objects in a system.*

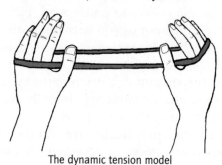

The dynamic tension model

When we have competing priorities in our lives, we often experience dynamic tension. This tension can manifest itself in a number of ways. A dynamic system is, in the first instance, potent, active and energetic. So when we have competing priorities we may feel challenged and excited. Our adrenalin may run high. We may think creatively and learn quickly. So dynamic tension can be beneficial, leading to creative and exciting results.

However, excessive tension can also contribute to a range of unwanted emotional and physical effects; effects such as stress, anxiety, dissatisfaction and worry. Unchecked, this tension can also lead to burn-out or feelings of helplessness.

When we understand that our lives are systems in dynamic tension, we can start to see creative new solutions.

TENSION DIAGRAMS

We can draw pictures of situations where we have competing priorities using a simple visual tool. We call this tool a *tension diagram*. A tension diagram shows the two opposing or contradictory states as *nodes*. These nodes represent the issues or activities that are in tension in our lives. The force that exists between the two nodes is represented by a *spring* which is in tension.

Node ● ——— (spring) ——— ● Node

Like the elastic band, the spring is not in balance. It is constantly trying to move and readjust. The more we pull one node away from the other, the more tension is stored in the spring. The more the nodes are moved closer together, the less tension is stored in the spring.

Let's now look at how we can use systems thinking and tension diagrams to shed new light on old problems.

Some familiar tensions

The tension between work and family is a common dilemma.

Work • ——— Family

Left unresolved, this dilemma can lead to increasing tension in our relationships. This tension can manifest itself in many ways, including problems with family members such as our partner or children, poor work performance or personal stress. Often we address this dilemma by attempting to spend more time with family or more time at work. This is the old "balance" approach. Often though, rather than solving the problem, this just transfers it from one area to the other. We start to spend more time with family to make up for our past over-attention to work. What can happen then is that our performance at work can slip.

> **The conflict between work and home is not just a conflict over time, but over values.**
>
> *Peter M. Senge*

This dilemma is often not simply solved by reallocating time. Any solutions that will work in the long term need to take our values and attitudes into account. Effective strategies to manage the tension between work and family will be discussed later in this book.

Another common area of tension lies in the dimensions of knowing, being and doing. These were discussed in chapter 1.

Doing

Being   Knowing

These dimensions can often be in tension in our lives. We may focus too heavily on knowing and doing, perhaps by working too hard or worrying too much, and ignore the "being" dynamic in life, perhaps in the form of relaxation and rest. Tension can then build up in the system. We may experience this tension as feeling mentally drained or it may strike in the form of stress-related physical problems.

Creating vs sustaining

Knowing, being and doing together represent one way to conceptualize our life experience. Another way is to think about the amount of personal energy we put into "creating" activities and "sustaining" activities.

"Creating" activities can include our work, bringing up our children or our hobbies. They are often activities that intrinsically provide us with pleasure, satisfaction or meaning. Conversely, "sustaining" activities include things like exercise, health care and mental relaxation. These sustaining activities support our long-term physical and mental well-being.

Systems thinking can help us think about how we use our personal energy on these two types of activities. We may also recognize a personal tension between these activities.

Creating • ——— ⟨⟨⟨⟨⟨⟨⟨⟩⟩⟩⟩⟩⟩⟩ ——— • Sustaining

This creating–sustaining tension is graphically illustrated in the lives of many artists. Artists like Michelangelo, Jackson Pollock and Janis Joplin each expended enormous amounts of personal energy creating their works at the expense of the sustaining aspects of their lives.

In our own lives, when creativity takes hold, sustaining ourselves can take a back seat. We work late into the night, or for days or months on end, directing all our energy towards our creative pursuits. Of course, this is not a bad thing that should be avoided. The creative drive in human beings is quite natural and can lead to great achievements. However, it can come at a cost both to ourselves and to those around us.

Conversely, when we focus our energy on sustaining activities, such as exercise or holidays, we may feel invigorated and full of life. Importantly, our sustaining activities can give us *more* energy to pursue our other interests. However, when we focus all our energy on sustaining activities it may reduce our creativity, making us bored and listless.

Ultimately, each of us needs to understand our own personal creativity–sustainability tension and manage it to achieve creativity while remaining aware of the potential costs.

Interestingly, this tension has been recognized for thousands of years and is portrayed in the Hindu religion in the forms of the gods Brahma the Creator and Vishnu the Sustainer. In fact, the Hindu religion defines a third type of energy in the form of Siva the Destroyer and Reproducer.

Freudians also refer to something similar in their discussions of *thanatos* or the death instinct. And, in fact, this third type of energy does play a role in the lives of many individuals. It can be seen in destructive behavior towards either ourselves or others.

Systems thinking and tension diagrams can also be applied to business and social issues. Let's look at some social examples.

One debate that often rages in our communities is between the advocates of free speech and the advocates of censorship. This social tension is managed through a broad range of approaches; film classification, for example, restricts access to certain movies, thereby acting as a form of censorship, while the American Bill of Rights enshrines people's right to free speech and liberty. When these competing priorities are not well managed we may see the excesses of racial vilification on one side or the extremes of political correctness on the other.

Free speech ● ——— ——— ● Censorship

Finally, another example of competing social priorities is the one between economic considerations and environmental concerns.

Economic ● ——— ——— ● Environmental
considerations   concerns

The current debates over sustainable development, greenhouse gas emission levels and the carbon tax are all examples of society's efforts to manage this tension better.

We will look at creative methods to manage these types of competing priorities later.

The chapters so far have concentrated on "knowing". Specifically, they have considered two related issues: redefining success to integrate it with soul, and thinking beyond balance to a systems approach to life.

The remaining chapters are about "doing". Together they are a road map for achieving success with soul. The emphasis is on building quality relationships, including the internal relationships between our mind, body and soul.

It's not hard and it's not mysterious. And while previous chapters have been mainly theoretical, the remainder of this book is practical and experiential.

The activities presented have been used by many people to achieve positive change in their lives. Although not widely published, many of these personal reflection methods have been utilized throughout the world. Other activities, like the personal values pyramid, are new and based on the latest international research.

Together they form a personal program you can use, either by yourself or, with slight modification, with others. Although the activities are written with the individual in mind, many of the comments and activities are relevant to families, groups and organizations, and to our relationships with others.

The methods and activities are "content-less". You provide the content from your own life experience. They focus on what is meaningful to you – not on your personality or on things like your preferred style of communication. They are also not proscriptive. They don't describe what you should or shouldn't be doing with your life.

Chapters 8 through 11 are about personal planning. They follow a natural progression, starting with a situational analysis: "How did I arrive at where I am now?" and "Where am I currently?" In building this picture of your past and present, you can create a firm basis on which to begin to answer the question: "Where am I going?"

Planning without action is a poor investment, so chapters 12 through 16 provide a set of practical activities to make it happen – to turn planning into action. They address the questions: "How do I start?" and "How do I get there?"

Finally, chapter 17 describes ways to be grounded and centered in what is meaningful to you. Here the focus shifts from knowing and doing, to being.

DOING

CHAPTER EIGHT

PERSONAL VALUES

S UCCESS IS CREATED through quality relationships with the self, with others and with our environment. These relationships are bound together by our thoughts and feelings and, underlying these, our values. Purpose in life, self-respect and quality relationships are most likely to be achieved when these values are clear.

> The years teach much that the days never know.
>
> *Ralph Waldo Emerson*

Our personal values develop from our personal beliefs. A *belief* is a conscious or subconscious proposition. For example, "I believe that all people are equal." Beliefs can be true or false, such as "the earth is round", strongly emotional ("violence is abhorrent") or moralistic ("gambling is bad").

Beliefs, as well as being stated, can also be inferred from what we do. They are expressed through our actions. For example, when we vote we express a belief that our preferred political party is the best party to govern the country.

Sometimes strong beliefs develop after a unique or unusual experience; for example, believing we saw a table levitate or having a near-death experience. However, most of our beliefs arise from our day-to-day experiences.

When beliefs are related to each other and are about a specific subject they are called *attitudes*. For example, when you hear all the beliefs a person holds about say, unions, you can conclude that the person has a positive or a negative attitude towards unionism.

Strongly held beliefs may also serve as enduring principles that guide our decisions and actions. When a belief becomes a guiding principle it is called a *value*. The term "value" is appropriate for these guiding principles because, when we value something, we hold it in high esteem. We consider it of *value*.

Our personal values can be guiding principles about either desirable *modes of behavior*, such as honesty, fairness, tolerance; or *goals* such as freedom, world peace, human dignity.

Values differ from attitudes in a number of ways. Values *transcend* specific objects and situations. In contrast, attitudes concern specific objects and situations. For example, a person may value world peace but still have the attitude that countries should be allowed to manufacture and sell weapons internationally.

In general, our values are more resistant to change than our attitudes. They are often directly tied to our self-esteem. If, for example, we value our public image highly, then we would be devastated in the face of a social disgrace.

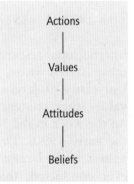

People often talk about their attitudes, but rarely about their values. This may be because our attitudes are specific, while our values are more general and less tangible. It is therefore easier to reveal our attitudes than our values. For example, it is relatively easy to discuss our attitudes to a question such as "Do you believe that the government should regulate against guns?" However, it can be quite difficult to decide whether we consider obedience or authority more important. Also, we may feel more comfortable revealing our attitudes because they reveal less about ourselves than our values do.

Our personal values incorporate past and present feelings, behaviors, experiences, thoughts and intentions. They are deeply ingrained personal standards which also determine our future directions and justify our past actions. And because values pertain to ways of behaving, or desirable goals, they also guide selection and evaluation of people and events.

Personal values affect all aspects of our experience and are inherent in all our endeavors and actions. Despite the diversity of human activities, whether it be endeavors such as managing employees, parenting children, buying a car or pursuing a leisure activity, the personal values underlying our actions derive from a small but enduring repertoire.

> Values which are shared and uplifting are followed effortlessly with passion from the heart.
>
> *Christo Norden-Powers*

THE LATEST RESEARCH

International researchers have closely examined values. Over the past few years, Dr Shalom Schwartz from the Hebrew University of Jerusalem has focused on specifying personal values, their content and structure. His work is based in part on the work in the 1970s by physiologist Milton Rokeach. In the early 1990s, Dr Schwartz conducted several studies on values. In the largest and most comprehensive work on values ever conducted, these studies have identified and verified fifty-seven personal values. Moreover, these values do not simply apply to one cultural group. They have been validated with hundreds of people across forty-four countries. This list of values is shown on the following page.

Schwartz's values list

Acceptance
Ambition
Authority
Beauty
Broadmindedness
Capability
Choosing your goals
Cleanliness
Country/Nation
Creativity
Curiosity
Daring
Devotion
Enjoyment
Environment
Equality
Excitement
Family
Forgiveness
Freedom
Friendship
Health
Helpfulness
Honesty
Honor
Humility
Independence
Influence
Inner harmony

Intelligence
Love
Loyalty
Meaning in life
Moderation
Nature
Obedience
Peace
Pleasure
Politeness
Privacy
Public image
Reciprocation of favors
Respect of tradition
Responsibility
Self-discipline
Self-indulgence
Self-respect
Sense of belonging
Social justice
Social order
Social power
Social recognition
Spirituality
Success
Variety
Wealth
Wisdom

Schwartz's research also shows these personal values cluster together into ten *motivational domains*. These motivational domains represent universal human goals that shape our behavior.

Ten motivational domains

Motivational domain	Values
Power	Social power, authority, wealth, public image, social recognition
Achievement	Capability, ambition, influence, intelligence, success
Hedonism	Pleasure, enjoyment, self-indulgence
Stimulation	Daring, variety, excitement
Self-direction	Curiosity, creativity, freedom, choosing own goals, independence, self-respect
Universalism	Environment, nature, beauty, broadmindedness, social justice, wisdom, equity, peace, inner harmony
Benevolence	Helpfulness, honesty, forgiveness, loyalty, responsibility, spirituality, friendship, love, meaning in life
Tradition	Acceptance, devotion, humility, respect for tradition, moderation, privacy
Conformity	Obedience, honor, politeness, self-discipline
Security	Cleanliness, country/nation, reciprocation of favors, social order, family, sense of belonging, health

HOW OUR VALUES DEVELOP AND CHANGE

Each of us develops a characteristic set of values that act as guiding principles in our lives. Our values set is hierarchical, with some values being more important than others. This values set develops and changes over time as we experience the interplay of our goals and desires. Thus, values derive from our experiences, especially novel and intense ones.

Both *internal* and *external* influences shape our values. Internal influences on our values include our developing view of how we would like others to see us and how we would like to see ourselves. These views include our preferred lifestyle, abilities, talents and feelings. External values may also be incorporated into our values set, particularly when significant people inspire or motivate us, or when others instill guilt or doubt in us.

Our values change as we move through life's developmental stages. Major events that occur during the pre-teen and early teenage years significantly shape our values. We are particularly receptive to external influences on our values when we are young or under stress or feeling vulnerable. Events such as war, technological developments and political upheavals can have a profound impact on a young person's developing values.

The formulation of our values is also affected by our *character* traits. For example, character traits such as perseverance or compassion are more likely to be found alongside values such as self-discipline and social justice.

Changes in personal values can be slow or sudden. Slow change occurs through continual challenges to behavior or beliefs. For example, challenges can come from a job change, new friends or media campaigns such as "smoking causes cancer" or "people shouldn't drink, then drive". The cumulative effect of these challenges can change our values.

Sudden changes to a person's values can occur after a significant event. Events such as divorce, natural disaster, sudden job loss, the death of someone close, serious disease, armed conflict and physical and psychological abuse can have a profound effect on personal values. People are particularly vulnerable to these events during their pre-teen and early teenage years as these are the formative years for the development of personal values.

The image we have of ourselves is, to a major extent, based on our values. In this way, personal values form the basic framework of who we think we are.

Bruce accepted a sales position with a large equipment manufacturer. The package included a good salary, a car, an opportunity to be his own boss and the chance to meet people. The attractiveness of the package influenced Bruce's decision to take the position. However, Bruce was to receive a weekly income based on volume and monetary value of sales. While he had no problem with this initially, later he came to consider this inconsistent with his personal values.

Every Monday the entire sales team met to review the previous week's sales figures, and a bonus would be awarded to the top salesperson. After several weeks, Bruce noticed that the other salespeople would look forward to the Monday sales meetings with a mixture of excitement and nervousness. He, on the other hand, only felt increasing discomfort as the weeks progressed. Bruce began to dread the moment the manager would go through the sales figures and he felt increasing pressure to perform in front of his peers. Competition went against Bruce's nature.

In his job, Bruce had initially enjoyed meeting his customers. But as his dislike for the weekly sales meetings increased, he found his attitude towards his customers changed. He began to focus solely on whether or not his customers purchased equipment, because this determined his income and affected how the sales manager treated him in the weekly meetings.

After several months, Bruce started to make up excuses for missing the sales meetings. He would be sick or purposely make an appointment to see a customer. One week he finally felt he stood at the crossroads: "Do I adopt the attitudes, behavior and values of the other salespeople, or do I resign?" Bruce decided to resign from his position.

Like Bruce, our personal values influence the career we choose, the interests we have and the people with whom we choose to spend our time. These choices may then reinforce and strengthen our own personal values.

Sometimes though, our values may be challenged as a result of the work we do and the values of the people with whom we interact. In these situations we may consciously or subconsciously adopt or reject the values associated with our work or with the people around us. In this way, we may "become what we do".

This interaction between personal values, career and social relationships is illustrated in Bruce's story. If Bruce had decided to stay in the sales position he either would need to change his values or he would experience stress due to the conflict between his values and the values associated with his job and workplace.

This is an example of the principle of *mutual causality*, where our values influence decisions, and these decisions in turn influence our values.

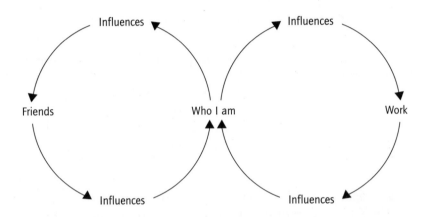

Friends can also influence our values. In some cases, they are a stronger influence on our values than other external factors, such as work. We can be more willing to conform to the social norms and values of our friends than to those of our work colleagues or other people around us.

The principle of mutual causality suggests that understanding our values and the values of our friends, our work and others around us, is an important personal skill. Having a clear understanding of our values, and the values of those around us, allows us consciously to determine those values we wish to cultivate, and those we do not.

> God protect me from my friends, I will take care of my enemies.
>
> *Hindu saying*

The principle of mutual causality also applies to the relationship between values, attitudes and actions. Values influence our attitudes, which in turn influence actions. In the same way, our actions influence attitudes and values.

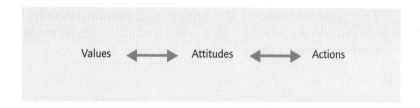

This concept is a potent and powerful tool for personal transformation. It says that *a new personal value can be adopted by behaving in ways consistent with that value.* Suppose, for example, we want to increase the personal value *responsibility*. First, we would identify opportunities where we could act responsibly. We would then ask ourselves, *"What would a responsible person do?" "What would be a responsible action in this situation, now?"* Once the action is identified, it could be implemented. In this way, responsible actions are incorporated into our behavioral repertoire and slow incremental changes will occur in our value system.

Another example of incremental change in responsibility can be seen when couples raise children. Prior to having children, the responsibilities of parenthood can only be imagined. When the child enters the family, parents incorporate the role of caregiver into their daily actions. This parental responsibility has a ripple effect on other aspects of the parents' lives, such as career and social activities. The new actions associated with the parental role result in a shift in the parents' values.

The reverse can also occur. We can decrease the importance of values by reducing actions associated with those values. In the example of parents, parental responsibilities decrease as children leave home. A major adjustment for parents occurs at this "empty nest" stage in the family cycle. Time spent in the parental caregiving role is replaced by other activities. Parents are confronted with the question, "What is important in my life now that the children are independent and have left home?"

STATED VERSUS ACTUAL VALUES

The thorny issue we all have with values is the difference between our *stated* values and the values which guide our actions – our *actual* values.

Stated values are the values we espouse. They are the values that we tell ourselves or our friends that we have. They may be our actual values, but sometimes they are the values we would *like* to have or display. They can also be values we admire in others or values we are told are "good".

When our actual values are inconsistent with the values of other people or organizations that we hold in high esteem, or when we act against our personal values, we may experience *dissonance*. This dissonance can manifest itself in guilt, anxiety, despair or alienation.

In the story we just looked at, Bruce experienced dissonance in his new sales job because he felt he had to act in ways that were inconsistent with his personal values.

Consistency between espoused and actual values is crucial for achieving success. This is accomplished through honest self-reflection and critical awareness of our own actual values and the values that guide those around us and, through them, the organizations to which we are affiliated.

Ian is an ambitious person who values environmental protection and social responsibility but also social power and public image. He is national president of a large, independent environmental protection organization. The group is actively lobbying government on waste disposal, endangered species and deforestation issues.

Ian knows that successful government lobbying requires a strong media voice and excellent government connections. He works to increase his influence and the respect he has among opinion leaders. He frequently talks at national and international conferences. He is positioned on relevant community and government advisory committees. He believes that influence and public recognition are the way to achieve his organization's objectives.

Ian is energetic and communicates in a direct and concise manner. This arises from his clear sense of purpose, and values which easily allow his behavior to be aligned with his espoused values. Ian can freely increase his influence without guilt or anxiety because he is acting consistently with who he really is and what he believes in.

Ian's story shows how values can be both consistent with career behavior and lead to a rich, fulfilling life. A clear value system, along with behavior that is consistent with those values, provides the bedrock for self-respect, purposeful goals in life, and intimate relationships with family, friends and the larger world.

DEFINING YOUR OWN PERSONAL VALUES

Let's now look at how you can identify your own personal values. This chapter has presented the latest research defining and specifying personal values. While only lists of "brain-stormed" values have previously been available, the research discussed in this chapter makes available a definitive set of fifty-seven personal values. With this new information, you can now look at your own personal values.

SOME SIMPLE STEPS TO BEGIN

The first thing to do is to look at the list of values on page 109 and tick the ten that you believe are most important as guiding principles in your life. Some may be more important than others, and we will go on to look at this later. Don't worry about it too much at this stage. Think about yourself as you are today. Go with your intuition. Don't labor over this task for too long. First reactions are probably best.

Now, think about the issue we just raised of stated versus actual values. It is likely that some of the values you have listed are actual values you hold but that others are really stated values. How do you know if your stated values are different from your actual values? To begin to work through this issue, you might find some of the following questions helpful:

- For each value I have listed, what is a recent situation in which I acted out of that value?
- Have any of my recent actions been inconsistent with those values? What did I feel as a result of an inconsistency between what I espoused and what I did?
- If someone else who didn't know me looked at the way in which I spend my time, what would they say are my actual values?
- Can some of my behavior be interpreted as arising from a value other than the one I think it is?
- Do I like the "idea" of holding any of these values, perhaps more than acting out of them?

Some of these are difficult questions to ask ourselves. Values go in and out of "fashion" and some of the values we hold may be quite different from those of the people around us. Sometimes it is difficult to admit even to ourselves that a value is one we hold. Similarly, sometimes we may have taken on the values around us so much that we don't even see they are out of alignment with who we really are.

Don't worry if you are not sure of the answers to these questions, or if you feel unclear about the distinction between your actual and stated values. There will be more activities looking at values in this chapter and the next one also. However, before moving on to some deeper work with your values, try the following activities.

- In which of the motivational domains on page 110 do your top ten values belong? What do the motivational domains tell you about what motivates you?
- As we have mentioned briefly, values are hierarchical. So another thing you can do is rank the values you have selected, from those which are most important to you, to those which are relatively less important. What are the

three values that are predominant guiding principles in your life? What attitudes do you have that are associated with each of your most important values?

CHARTING YOUR OWN PERSONAL VALUES

Personal reflection is a powerful learning tool, especially when it is structured. While working in India, we learned a method for personal reflection that we often use to reflect on a period of time or an event.

This method ensures that all aspects of a reflection are included – thoughts, feelings, objective facts – as well as the implications and decisions that might arise from the reflection.

This personal reflection activity – the *personal journey timeline* – has been adapted to help you clarify your personal values. The personal journey timeline will help you discover the values that have shaped your attitudes and behaviors and how those values may have changed over time.

Allow at least fifteen minutes to complete the activity. As you begin, it is important to keep a couple of points in mind. First, remember that there may be a real, or apparent, discrepancy between espoused and actual values. For example, I may say I am benevolent (espoused values) while my behavior might indicate that I am ambitious (actual value). Secondly, the values underlying a particular action can be quite different. Identical actions by two people can be motivated by totally different values. So think clearly about your own personal motivations and intentions.

To start with, draw up the following chart.

Title	
Key life changes	
Major changes	
Years	
Events/Happenings	
Mood High Low	
Values	

STEPS TO CREATING YOUR PERSONAL JOURNEY TIMELINE

Now follow the steps below to construct your own personal journey timeline.

1 *Years line.* Divide the year line into equal time segments that correspond with your entire life from birth to today. Mark in the years.

2 *Events line.* Below the years line, write the major significant *events* in your life. The events may be specific turning points or decisions. The events should be objective. Use a few words to capture the essence of each event.

3 *Mood line.* Identify the *emotions* (for example sadness, anger, grief, joy, terror, elation) associated with each event. Draw in a *mood* line that shows your feelings during each period. Continue the mood line to the present.

4 *Values.* Consider the values that have been important during different events in your life. Use the values on page 109 to select those which correspond to each section below the mood line.

5 *Major changes*. Mark your timeline at *three to six* major points that correspond to important events and/or shifts in values on your timeline. Give each section a short title. Let the title capture the essence of what was happening in your life at that time. Titles can be descriptive or emotional.

6 *Key life changes*. Next, divide your timeline into *two* key life segments with one major transition point. Use a vertical line to indicate the major transition point. Title the two sections. If it is important, you can use three sections.

7 *Title*. Create an overall title for your life. This could follow the statement, "The journey of my life is like …" or you may use a poetic or descriptive title.

You have completed a pictorial image of your life, a personal journey timeline. On page 121 there is an example of a completed one for a person named Karen.

If you wish, consider the following questions after you have completed your timeline:

- What surprised you as you completed your timeline?
- Was the activity easy?
- Do major events center on a particular aspect of your life (for example work, family, home, hobbies, relationships)?
- What are the main factors or events associated with your *mood* line?
- Look at the major changes. Was there a corresponding change in values at these times?
- What do you believe caused changes in your values?
- What were the internal and external factors associated with any changes in values that might have occurred?
- What decisions or changes in actions corresponded to your changes in values?
- What values would you like to change?
- How can you change your values?
- What methods have you used in the past to change your values?

This method can be adapted to consider a shorter period such as a week, a month or a year, or you can make a timeline based on a particular aspect of your life such as a sporting activity or your career.

Karen

Surfing the Waves of Change

Title	Surfing the Waves of Change				
Key life changes	Gaining the Confidence		Growth and Crisis		Renewal
Major changes	Early childhood	School	Finding myself as an adult	Major transitions	Second chance
Years	1955 1960	1973	1978 1984 1985	1990	1993 1994 1995 1996 1997
Events/Happenings	Born Pre-school School	High School Swimming Team ⊢Dated Paul ⊢College⊣	Graduation Graduation *1st job *2nd job *Met Michael *Thomas born *Married	move to West Coast *Separation *Met Andrew	*Remarry *Julie born
High / Low Mood					
Values	Family Curiosity	Excitement Intelligence Self-indulgence	Love Ambition Wealth	Health Responsibility Independence	Love Inner harmony Acceptance Belonging Family

121

BUILD YOUR VALUES PYRAMID

As previously mentioned, values are hierarchical. They can be visualized as a pyramid. Creating a personal *values pyramid* will help you clarify your values, formulate goals and set priorities.

At the top of the pyramid are a few very important personal values. These core values serve as the primary guiding principles in life and are closely tied to self-esteem – the level of positive regard we have for ourselves.

More values appear at the base of the pyramid. These values are less important than those at the top and play a secondary role in decision-making. The following is a values pyramid for a thirty-nine-year-old man. Three more examples of values pyramids are shown on pages 123–24.

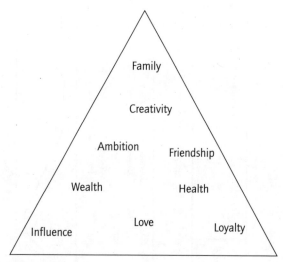

Charlie – 39 years old

You can create your own values pyramid using the values you selected in one of the previous activities in this chapter. Before you start, be sure they are current *actual* values – not values you would *like* to hold (espoused values).

To begin with, select two or three core values which have guided your actions throughout your life. These core values have played an important role in most decisions you have made. Look at your personal journey timeline and check the relative importance of each value and place the values in the pyramid. The most important two or three values are at the top. If two values are of equal importance they can be placed on the same level to show this.

Select three or four values that are next in importance and place them in the middle of the pyramid. These may include values that you have incorporated into your life over the past few years. If two values are equally important, again, place them on the same level.

Finally, place your remaining values in the lower third of the pyramid. These values may relate to current issues or interests. A number of the values near the base of the pyramid may be on the same level.

This drawing now represents your current values pyramid. You may wish to compare your values pyramid with those on pages 123–24. Each of these values pyramids represents people with contrasting sets of values.

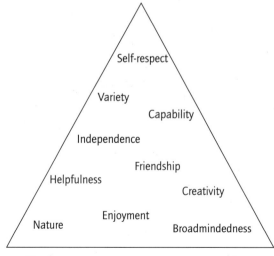

Ian – 35 years old

Rita – 27 years old

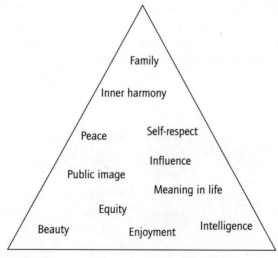

Wendy – 45 years old

Using this method you can also develop values pyramids for different times in your life. It can be interesting and useful to compare how your values have changed over time. Your values pyramid can also help you to predict how you might feel if a particular decision or action is taken.

In this chapter, we have looked in some detail at what personal values are, how those values change and the difference between stated and actual values. We have also seen how we can identify our own personal values and determine those which are most important to us by creating our own values pyramid. With this knowledge we can now look at what provides us with personal meaning.

CHAPTER NINE

LIFE DESIGN

PERSONAL VALUES, along with our experiences and personality, are the foundations on which we build success with real meaning. You now perhaps have a better understanding of your personal values, and are ready to take the next step – to define the dimensions of your life that are important and meaningful to you.

> Each object is much more than it seems to be. The key to its meaning is in what those who made it said about it, how they used it, and how together they behaved towards it.
>
> *Smithsonian Institution*

These dimensions will form the building blocks from which to construct your life's purpose and develop your personal strategic plans. In this way, these dimensions will define what success and soul mean to you. If you found the previous chapter's discussion of personal values somewhat vague or abstract, we think you will find identifying what's important and meaningful to you much more tangible and concrete.

As we have discussed previously, each person constructs meaning in different ways. What is important and meaningful for one person may not be important and meaningful for someone else. Similarly, what provides soul for one person may lack soul for someone else. So, rather than being prescriptive here, we have provided a method which allows each person to define for themselves what is important and meaningful.

Your key content areas

There may be many aspects of your life which are important and meaningful to you. They may be your family, friends, job, hobbies, places you visit, things you do and so on. We call these various aspects or dimensions *key content areas*.

What does this term mean? First, *key* implies something fundamental. It also suggests unlocking something for you, some meaning perhaps. Next, *content*, because you bring your personal content to that dimension. For example, your content might include your skills, energy and commitment. And finally *area*, because each dimension covers a part of your life, like an area of ground or terrain.

How can we define these key content areas? What might a key content area be for you?

One way to identify these areas, of course, is to look at how much *time* we devote to different activities. For example, you might say your key content areas are your work, family or partner, the gym, sleep, and so on.

Books on time-management often use this approach. They have to because they are helping us prioritize and allocate our time among the various activities we do.

But defining what's important and meaningful on this basis alone is inappropriate. First, what is meaningful is not always related to time. For example, the house in Italy where her father grew up is meaningful to Doris, but she currently spends almost no time there; in fact, she has rarely spent much time there at all. Conversely, although an hour a day in traffic getting to and from work may be necessary, it is usually not considered very meaningful. Secondly, this time-based approach is boring and unimaginative. It lacks creativity and flexibility. Most people don't want to define their lives in terms of a limiting concept such as the hours in a day, week or year. Finally, defining your life in terms of your time operates out of the old balanced lifestyle model, where you worry about spreading your time over a range of activities. As we know, this is not the path to success with real meaning.

Another common way to define the important dimensions of our lives is to think about our *roles*. These may be roles such as parent, manager, community member, son or daughter, teacher or student. When we think about our roles, we also tend to think about our responsibilities in each of those roles, such as demonstrating leadership, setting a good example, doing what's expected of us, and so on.

This way of defining the important dimensions of our life is also limited. Again, it does not necessarily address the issue of personal meaning. Many things which people find meaningful fall outside traditional roles. For example, collecting and playing blues records provides Stephen with personal meaning, but he doesn't see himself having a "role" as a record collector.

Another way to select our key content areas would be to base them on our *skills or talents*. For example, we may have skills in child raising, tennis, consulting, teaching and so on. However, most people have a very broad range of skills and talents, more than they will ever use to their full capacity. They would, therefore, possibly have hundreds of key content areas to satisfy.

Certainly, skills and talents are important. We use our skills and talents on activities we find meaningful and important, like an artist using her painting and drawing skills to express herself. In this way, *our skills and talents may support what is important and meaningful*. They are, therefore, a "means to an end", rather than an end in themselves.

So what are our key content areas likely to be? Put simply, they are things that are meaningful to us. They may be things we feel passionate about. They may be things that we understand deeply or care about a great deal. They are things we consider important or necessary.

Shane is a structural geologist. He works for a large resource company which flies him around the world as a consultant to the company's various mines. Often these mines are located in remote parts of the world, like the jungles of Borneo, the deserts of Australia and Africa, the mountains of Peru. Shane enjoys all the travel.

Being a structural geologist, Shane understands how mountains and valleys are created from the stresses which build up in the earth's crust. When he looks out the window he sees it all laid out before him – the grand patterns of nature. Sitting next to Shane in a light plane heading for some remote part of the world is always a wonderful experience, hearing the passion with which he describes the landforms and the dynamics that formed them. It is hard to imagine Shane doing any other job. He loves the one he has so much, and part of the reason it means so much to him is his deep understanding and wonderment of nature.

Clearly, one of Shane's key content areas is his work, although he may think of it more as a personal interest which he is paid to pursue. Shane is like a lot of people who work in an area they are passionate about. They don't consider what they do as work. They love doing it because it provides them with meaning.

> We go to work not only for our daily bread, but for our daily meaning.

Your key content areas could also include important *relationships*. For example, our key content areas include our parents, friends and work colleagues. These are the people we are close to and who share many of our values. Other relationships, which people might define as key content areas, could be their relationship with God or to a special place, maybe the one where they grew up.

DEFINING YOUR KEY CONTENT AREAS

With these thoughts in mind you can now define your own key content areas. All you need is some quiet time, a pen or pencil and paper. Start by writing down what's important to you. Think about:

- What do I do?
- What's important to me?
- What am I passionate about?
- What has meaning or provides me with meaning?
- What do I spend my energy or time on?
- What are the important relationships in my life?
- In what aspects of my life do I wish to be successful?

When thinking about these questions, concentrate on your current situation. Your key content areas should be based on where your life is at the present moment.

Remember, because we define soul as that dimension of ourselves concerned with meaning, your key content areas should acknowledge soul. In addition, your key content areas should be dimensions in which you want to have success.

When you have formulated these initial ideas, aim for, say, between four and twelve key content areas. Your key content areas could include a range of things – objects, places, activities, people, locations, relationships. Whatever is meaningful to you. If you come up with many more than twelve, try to group similar things together. For example, you may wish to group hobbies.

When defining your key content areas you may also wish to think of creative names for each of them, names that really bring out the meaning in that key content area for you. Redefine that part of your life that involves making money. For example, work might be "making a difference to the environment" or "creating the best workforce that I can". It doesn't have to be labeled just "work". The title you give each key content area should be as personal and meaningful to you as possible. What is it really about for you? A friend of ours works for a photographic company in developing new digital technology. He calls his job "Creating the future way of life". He is *that* excited about it.

Remember, you don't need to include all your roles or skills or all the things you spend time doing. There are no set answers; if your car is that important to you, make it a key content area.

As you are thinking about your key content areas, look back over the personal values you identified in chapter 8. Your personal values and key content areas should make sense together – they should be consistent. For example, if you define environment and nature as important personal values, then some of your key content areas might be camping or environmental activism. Alternatively, if you defined some of your personal values to be daring, variety and excitement, you might include activities like scuba diving, paragliding and rock climbing as key content areas.

Are your values consistent with your key content areas? If they are not, you may want to think about how you could modify your key content areas or your personal values to bring them into alignment.

Give each of your key content areas a name or phrase to describe it. As mentioned, think up creative names or phrases to describe each of them. The important thing is that they mean something to you. Remember this chapter is called "Life Design"; you have the skills and the insights to design your own life.

YOUR LIFE CIRCLE

Using these dimensions of your life you can create a picture – a picture which contains all your key content areas. To do this, draw a circle, then fill it in with a segment for each of your key content areas. Make them slices or segments, like those of a birthday cake. We call this circle your current *life circle* because it represents your life, with all the important and meaningful parts at present.

To help you we have included a few examples. The first is a life circle drawn by a teenager Doris recently spoke with.

Next, a farmer might define his life circle like the one below. Many of his key content areas may relate to his farm.

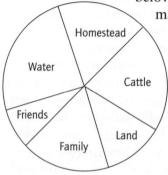

A professional golfer might have only two key content areas: golf and everything else. The golfer may spend 12–15 hours a day working on his game, and he may well spend a great deal of the rest of his waking hours thinking about golf too.

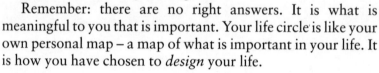

Remember: there are no right answers. It is what is meaningful to you that is important. Your life circle is like your own personal map – a map of what is important in your life. It is how you have chosen to *design* your life.

LIFE CIRCLES AND CREATIVITY

Life circles are creative tools for exploring what your life is all about. They don't require writing lists or keeping an extensive journal. Once you have decided on your current key content areas you can do a lot with them, just by "playing" with the life circle idea. Over the next few pages there are a variety of activities to try.

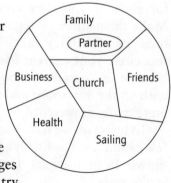

You can think creatively about how the different dimensions might fit together and what shape to make each of them. Rather than making them all wedges, like a pie, you might try using different shapes and sizes.

Alternatively you can take one or more of your key content areas and divide them into a number of other key content areas. For example, let's have a look at how the professional golfer might divide up their "golf" key content area.

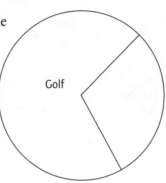

Using this method you could create a complex network of linked and interconnected life circles for the various dimensions of your life – a network with a central life circle and a series of "satellite" circles projecting out and perhaps linking together.

Life circles are *perceptual maps*. They allow us to create a picture of our lives which is both orderly and chaotic – representing our life *system*. These maps can create a rich pattern, with each circle forming a fractal, and a whole series of interconnected circles forming a complex pattern where each circle develops out of another.

Life circles are also an important *systems thinking* tool. They show the components, connections and relationships that are important to us. They describe and encode personal meaning in a simple visual form. Importantly, these perceptual maps are not a static representation of your life. They change and evolve over time as do our lives. New key content areas develop while others may disappear or evolve into something different.

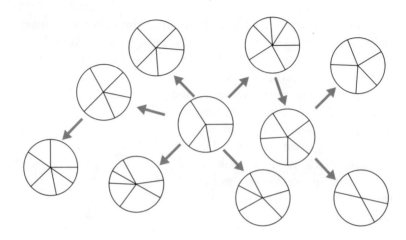

You can also use these systems thinking tools in a business or organisational context. They can help you to think about the important dimensions of your business or department. For example, your key content areas for your business might include customers, suppliers, your employees, all of your offices or buildings, and so on. Or they might include different aspects of your work such as consulting, research, maintenance, manufacturing and so on.

One further activity you may wish to try: consider the amount of time you spend on each of your key content areas. Redraw your life circle with each slice or segment drawn in proportion to the amount of time you *currently spend* on it. Then draw another circle based on the amount of time you would *like to spend* on each key content area. Compare the two circles. Consider what you could do to move from your current life circle to your preferred life circle. Make a list of strategies for change if you wish.

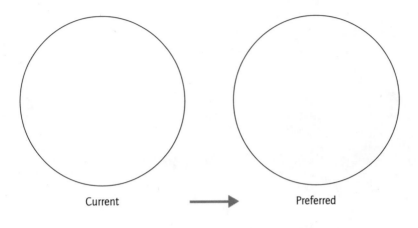

Current   ⟶   Preferred

Strategies for change

_____

_____

_____

_____

_____

_____

Life circles provide a powerful, flexible framework for thinking about the present and planning for the future. Having now used life circles to draw our lives in the present, we will go on to use these life circles for thinking about the future in the chapter on personal strategic planning. But first, let's move on to thinking about your life's purpose.

CHAPTER TEN

DEFINING YOUR
LIFE'S PURPOSE

Meaning or purpose serves as a point of reference. As long as we keep purpose in focus in both our organizational and private lives, we are able to wander through the realms of chaos, make decisions about what actions will be consistent with our purpose, and emerge with a discernible pattern or shape to our lives.

Margaret Wheatley

Doris's first employer, Jordan, expected a lot from people, sometimes more than they were able to give. He ran a successful research company specializing in customer service research and although he wasn't perfect, he had clearly thought a great deal about life. On the other hand, at that time, Doris was a recent graduate ready to take on the world.

On one occasion Doris was designing a piece of research to address one of their clients' customer service issues. She hadn't been with the company long and wanted to impress her new boss, so she rushed in as young people sometimes do and designed the research assuming she would use a questionnaire to interview customers about their attitudes. Well, she was stopped in her tracks pretty quickly when she met with the boss to discuss the approach she had taken. "What do you mean by 'attitudes'?" he started off with. And then, "What's your *model*?" "Model? What model? I don't have a model," she replied, embarrassed and confused, having no idea what he was talking about.

He went on to explain: "We all operate out of a model, whether we recognize it or not. And, in this case, you should know the model you are using. But you say you don't have a model. That's where you're wrong. You do have a model, but you don't know what it is. So how can you know if it's the right model if you are not even conscious of it?"

Doris was pretty shocked by how little she knew. But she also realized she had just learned an important lesson about work, and about life. We all operate out of a model of what life is about whether we know it or not.

One of the important models out of which we operate is our life's purpose – a model of what our life is about, what the point of it is.

By the word "purpose", we mean it in its biggest sense – *the reason why we exist*. Take a simple example. What is the purpose of a hammer? The purpose of a hammer is to drive nails into timber. This is why the hammer has been created. Similarly, each of us exists for a purpose. This purpose is our *life's purpose*. However, unlike the hammer, our purpose is made up of two components:

• what life demands from us
• what we demand from life.

In other words, our life's purpose is defined by *our response to life and life's response to us*.

Whether we have consciously determined our life's purpose or not, *we are all operating out of a life's purpose*. We are living every day, making decisions and choices, and every one of these decisions and choices says something about our purpose in life – every one. Paradoxically, this is an old idea; that we are measured by our actions. And it is true – our life's purpose is measurable by our actions.

Just like a researcher operating out of a model they haven't articulated clearly to themselves – let alone to others – we are living our life's purpose whether we are aware of it or not, and whether we like it or not. What can be even more frightening is that sometimes our life's purpose is clearer to others – through our actions – than it is to ourselves...

A former work colleague of Doris's likes others to think of him as generous and charitable. Whenever he makes a donation to a good cause he makes sure everyone knows about it. However, the thing people notice most about him is not what he tells them. What they notice is his expensive clothes, his fancy car; in short, they notice how much time and money he spends on…himself.

Some people say this can't be true – they can't be operating out of a purpose because they haven't worked out what their life's purpose is yet. They are working it out and they will do it when they have worked it out. This is commonly heard today and it is often supported by a society which says it's okay to be uncertain, to have not decided. However, we call this attitude "the Bombay cab ride" approach to life…

> Who you are speaks so loudly I can't hear what you're saying.
>
> *Ralph Waldo Emerson*

THE BOMBAY CAB RIDE

We love India. We have enjoyed it and struggled in it many times. It frustrates, enthralls and teaches us. One of the many special experiences in India is the Bombay cab ride.

The cabs of Bombay are little, old-fashioned cars, painted black with a yellow roof, and they make up about half the traffic in the city. The cars are Morris Oxfords, circa 1950s model. This is the model still rolling off the production line today in India. They are very English, and they literally trundle around the hopelessly crowded streets of Bombay. Of course, that the traffic moves at all is a miracle. That you can get to your destination without an accident is a testament to the skill and experience of Bombay's many cab drivers.

To enhance the Bombay cab ride experience, some drivers like to make a little extra money from tourists using an old trick: "Sorry sir, meter is broken," they explain, wobbling their heads from side to side in a uniquely Indian way. If the meter is "broken", the appropriate fare cannot be calculated and, if a fare is not agreed upon before departing, the taxi driver will decide what is a "reasonable" fare at your final destination.

Some people are like this with their lives. They say they cannot be measured on what is happening at the moment, because they "haven't figured out what their life's purpose is yet". This sounds like a "broken" meter. The meter is broken so the journey is not being measured. However, whether the meter is "broken" or not, the journey is happening and the worth of the journey can be made assessed at the other end.

We may claim that "the meter is broken" in our lives, that we haven't figured out our life's purpose yet, but the reality is that we are traveling on life's road somewhere and somehow, and often we choose the road *and* the direction. It is as if every step is being recorded on videotape. At the end of the journey, what has happened has happened. If someone had been following us around the whole time, they would have seen it. The reality is that a lot of people do see it.

For some people, the search for a life's purpose becomes an end in itself; the journey is more important than reaching the destination. There is nothing wrong with this for a while. We may well need to spend some time *actively* developing our understanding of our life's purpose. However, being or thinking alone rarely results in an answer to this question. Sitting and waiting to be summoned for some important job that only you can do usually doesn't work. It generally only provides an excuse for inaction.

"Doing" is what is also required to make our life's purpose clear. Getting out there and doing something is more likely to result in some answers than "being" and "knowing" alone.

Before going on to explore ways in which life's purpose can be defined, let's look at ways in which some people look at their life's purpose.

There are people who can clearly articulate their life's purpose. Doris's mother will tell you, in no uncertain terms, that her purpose is to look after her immediate family – her husband, her two children and the partners of her children. She is a strong woman who also contributes significantly to people outside that circle. However, she is very clear in her own mind that charity begins at home.

For some people their life's purpose may be their job, country, community or a combination of these things. For others who are sure of their life's purpose, a crisis can occur that leads them to question themselves. This often seems to happen in midlife – the "what am I doing with my life?" question arises. This is life demanding something from us, challenging us to think again about what our lives are about.

Still others argue that there is no purpose to life, that it is actually meaningless. Today this view is frequently expressed by young people disillusioned by the values of their elders – they see these values graphically illustrated in the degradation of their world by previous generations.

Finally, some people say they don't know how to determine their life's purpose. They would like to, if only they knew how to work it out. Methods to do just that follow in the remainder of this chapter. But first of all, think about what you would say in the following situation:

An alien spaceship has just landed near where you live. You walk outside and stand there, dumbfounded as the shiny spaceship opens and a small humanoid figure walks out. It looks around at the landscape before it turns its attention to you.

The alien, deciding you are probably the smartest thing around at the moment, walks up to you and says, "What are you on this planet for?" From the look in the alien's inquiring eyes, it is going to be disappointed if you don't have a half-reasonable answer. And you will most likely be too stunned at this point to make up an answer on the spot. So, before any aliens turn up unexpectedly, let's get your answer ready.

This answer – your life's purpose – should be full of your own personal meaning. It not only comes from your head and your heart. It comes from your soul, the seat of inner meaning. Your life's purpose acts as your compass, it guides your decisions and choices. It is defined internally, then finds its expression through your words and actions and in your interaction and relationship with the world.

Often people talk about life's purpose in the singular, as if each individual has one clear unitary purpose in their life. This may well be so; certainly many theologians and philosophers have expounded this view. But how closely does this reflect our life experience and the way in which we currently talk about our lives?

Our experience as we talk to people about the various dimensions of meaning in their lives is that *most people gain meaning from a range of life experiences*. They may also wish to achieve a range of personal objectives: to be a good parent, to have good friends or to live a long life, for example. Sometimes a person may even have a number of objectives focused in one particular dimension of their lives – their work, for example.

So how do we reconcile our current reality with the age-old idea of one person–one purpose? Is it that, in the current age, we have somehow "got it wrong"? Or are we just waiting for our one unifying life purpose to become clear to us? These are deep and difficult questions.

The fact of the matter is that there may be a great deal of purpose in our lives – across a range of areas. Rather than worrying that our lives may lack a single central purpose, the approach we recommend is *to work with what is given and build on that reality*. This is a meaningful and purposeful way for each individual to begin to address some of these issues.

Remember also that your life's purpose should not be solely based on your skills or what you are good at. It is what means something to you that is important, not what you can do well. Meaning is the most important dimension.

VALUES, EXPERIENCES AND LIFE DIMENSIONS

Our life's purpose develops out of our personal values, our social and cultural environment, our personal experiences, our personality and our soul. The previous two chapters examined these issues. They considered the following questions:
- Where have I been?
- Who am I?
- What is important to me?
- What provides me with meaning?

By answering these questions you have already started the process of thinking about your life's purpose.

We often arrive at an understanding of our life's purpose through our experience. In chapter 8 you developed your personal journey timeline. This activity was designed to help you reflect on your life experiences, how you responded to those experiences and what meaning they held for you.

In addition, your life's purpose should be *aligned* with your personal values and what motivates you. Therefore, reviewing these values is also helpful to start you thinking about your life's purpose. One of the activities in chapter 7 enabled you to draw a values pyramid, identifying the values that are important to you. As a thought starter, it may be helpful to revisit that values pyramid.

You can take this initial activity a little further by thinking about which motivational domains your personal values are located in. The motivational domains which hold all of the values are listed on page 110. Using your pyramid, write down beside your pyramid your motivational domains ranked from most important at the top to least important at the bottom. An example is shown on page 147. If you have not drawn a values pyramid, you can simply think about the values and motivational domains that apply to you and try to rank them.

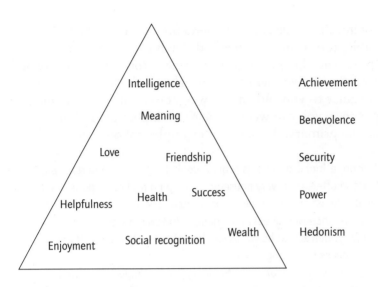

STATEMENTS OF PURPOSE

Now let's build on your *personal experiences*, as depicted in your personal journey timeline, and *values*, as displayed in your values pyramid. In chapter 9 you defined your key content areas – those aspects, people, places and relationships that are important to you. These are the dimensions of meaning in your life, so they should form part of your life's purpose – or, put another way, each of them should have a purpose. Therefore we will use these key content areas as a basis for developing your life's purpose.

Your life's purpose can be defined by a series of statements, one statement for each of your key content areas. These statements are called *statements of purpose* and they are not specific goals or achievements, they are about *intent*. They illustrate why you have included the key content area in your life circle. Each statement can stand on its own. In this way your life's purpose is complete because it includes a statement for every dimension of meaning in your life.

Some people may not be satisfied with having a series of statements to define their life's purpose. They may feel that, for them, there needs to be one defining life purpose. This is possible, too, using this method. Each of your statements of purpose can be given a weighting. You can rank them differently or give them equal weightings if they are of equal importance to you. When you weight each of your statements of purpose, you can weight one much higher than all the rest. It can be primary. A couple of examples follow.

> Wilson, a friend of ours, is a great cook. He loves to entertain and does so often. He is very houseproud, keeping his home spotless and neat. He is also very family-orientated, spending time with his parents whenever he gets the chance. However, the most important thing for him is that he writes children's books. He is a writer and he sees this as his calling in life.
>
> Another friend of ours, Marlene, has a range of activities in which she participates. She works part-time, is studying a course in computer science and, in between, loves to relax or go out with her friends. Her life's purpose is about getting by in life, supporting herself, getting some mental stimulation, being a good friend, a good partner and enjoying life as much as she can along the way.

Getting your thoughts clear for each statement of purpose can take time. It is not easy. One way to start is to select an easier key content area. If you are currently not so clear about certain key content areas, it may be best to start with another key content area. Leave the others until later, when you have gained some experience writing your statements.

Here are some useful suggestions which may help you:
- Make your statements of purpose simple; complex ideas or words are generally less helpful.
- Aim for about one or two sentences for each statement. Brevity will give each of your words more importance and meaning. Spend some time getting the wording right.
- Be creative – make your statements sound positive, interesting and appealing.
- If you find yourself mixing too many ideas together, chances are you should break a key content area into two separate areas with a separate statement of purpose for each.

- Don't forget to look back at your personal values and think about what they say about your statements of purpose and what your statements of purpose say about your values. Statements of purpose that are not aligned with your personal values will probably seem hollow and meaningless. You may also wish to revise your personal values based on your statements of purpose. In this way, your personal values, key content areas and statements of purpose can inform each other and you can create alignment among them.

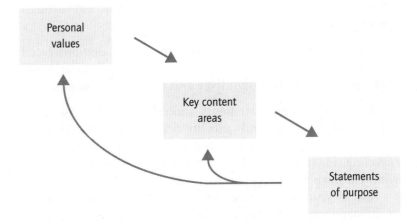

- Don't worry if some of the individual statements of purpose contradict each other. This can happen. Don't try to resolve these contradictions here, just note them and let them stand. We will examine strategies for managing these competing priorities or contradictions later, in chapter 13.
- Finally, remember your statements of purpose are not specific goals or achievements; they describe why you have included that key content area in your life circle in the first place.

Don't be concerned if you can't write your statements of purpose straight off. Most people can't. They find it easier to make some notes or a list and then piece their statements together from those. You can also develop your statements of purpose with your partner or family.

For reference, here are some examples of our key content areas and statements of purpose.

Home... To provide a warm and friendly domestic environment that is welcoming and functional and reflects the personalities and interests of the occupants. In short, an aural and visual feast.

Career... To enhance personal and organizational effectiveness through the provision of quality consulting, counselling and training services.

Friends... To enrich our lives and the lives of others through friendship.

Contribution to others... To provide an active, demonstrated contribution to the well-being of the wider community; one that enriches both our own lives and the lives of others.

If possible, your statements should fit on one piece of paper. Write them around your life circle if you wish. You can keep your statements of purpose with you at work or when traveling. Having them close at hand can help to remind you what they are and keep you focused.

Just as your key content areas can change over time, so your statements of purpose can change. Different experiences, both external and internal, can realign your statements. This may happen when you change your job, turn forty, buy a house, get married or have children, travel, or perhaps if you go through a separation or lose something or someone significant. Major life transitions are often good times for questioning or modifying your statements of purpose. Just as your life is an on-going "work in progress", your statements of purpose are also an on-going "work in progress". They may never be completed to your

> Constantly to seek the purpose of life is one of the odd escapes of man. If he finds what he seeks it will not be worth that pebble on the path.
>
> *J. Krishnamurti*

150

total satisfaction but then they are enduring and developing like your life system.

Next you can use these key content areas and statements of purpose to develop your personal strategic plan. In this way, your statements of purpose will be the springboard to the remainder of your life. They will be the foundation on which you will build your long-term plans.

CHAPTER ELEVEN

PERSONAL
STRATEGIC PLANNING

> The best way to predict the future is to create it.
>
> *Peter Drucker*

Ivan parked the car in the driveway. He'd been away for a few days on a business trip. "Funny," he thought, "Teresa's car is not here." He opened the front door and walked inside. A note was sitting on the small table in the hallway. He put his suitcase down and read it. Teresa had packed her bags, including the children's things, and left him. The note said she and the children had gone to live at her mother's place across town. Ivan sat down in the kitchen. He felt dazed and disappointed – how could this have happened?

Many years ago at college, Ivan had studied accounting. Two years into his course a friend had offered him a job at an insurance company. The job paid well, included a car and involved some inter-state travel. Although he was doing well at college, Ivan decided to take the job.

Suddenly he had money to spend, while his college friends were delivering pizzas in the evenings for small change. His sales position paid good commissions and he had weekends off. With no study to do he was free to go fishing and camping, both of which he enjoyed very much.

After several years of work, Ivan met Teresa. She was working in the superannuation section of the company and they shared an interest in camping and traveling. After dating for a while they went on a trip to the Rockies together and there they fell in love.

After a short engagement, Ivan and Teresa were married and, with their two incomes, were able to buy both a nice house near where they worked, and a brand new recreational vehicle for week-end trips away. Things went well for a few years. By paying the minimum repayments on the house and the car, they found they could afford interesting holidays to places like Mexico and Hawaii.

However, when the economic recession hit in the late 1980s, Teresa's hours of work were cut from five to three days a week. Although they had not planned to have a family quite so early on, it seemed like a good time to start. Ivan's job was still going well. Teresa could take some time off work altogether, then go back to work three days a week while her mother took care of their child.

But Teresa had twins and taking care of them was a far bigger job than she had ever expected. Going back to work was simply out of the question. There was so much to do. Her mother spent most of her time helping Teresa anyway.

As the recession worsened, Ivan found making sales was tougher and he no longer made the same commissions they had come to rely on. All the money he earned was spent on the repayments on the house and all the bills. They had to sell the four-wheel drive and buy a cheaper car for Teresa.

Ivan talked to his friends about other jobs around town but conditions were difficult everywhere. Ivan's lack of qualifications didn't help, and now he wished he had finished college. Ivan also talked to his boss about the problems he was having with money. His boss was sympathetic and said he would see if there were any other opportunities in the company. After several weeks, Ivan's boss found him a well-paying job in the national sales team. However, it involved a great deal of travel.

Ivan thought it was a great opportunity. He could travel more frequently, which he liked to do, and they would be able to keep up the repayments on the house, which was beginning to look doubtful. "It will only be for a while," he told Teresa.

That was eighteen months before Teresa took the children and walked out.

In his landmark book *Future Shock*, Alvin Toffler discusses strategies for surviving in a world of rapid and increasing change. He notes that "few individuals or families plan ahead systematically".

By contrast, most organizations regularly conduct planning sessions. Senior executives and managers take a few days or a week away from the office to work out what the company should do with its products, people and services. In some companies, those who are required to act on these plans are also involved in this process.

Rarely do we question the wisdom of this approach. We take it for granted that this planning process is an important part of running a corporation. Shareholders and stakeholders want to know how resources are to be used and the company must chart a course to maintain or improve its competitive position. In this way, organizations recognize the link between structured, strategic management approaches and business success.

The link many people don't seem to make is that it's the same with personal success. Achieving significant and sustainable personal success also requires goal-setting and planning – not just at work, where we are paid to do it, but also in our personal lives. But how often do we use these principles in our own lives? For most of us the answer is – rarely.

So if we look at what organizations call "effective planning" we may find some useful approaches and strategies for our own personal planning.

In general, organizations consider planning effective if it:
- is structured
- generates achievable and measurable outcomes with a defined timeline for completing those outcomes
- involves those who will be required to act on the plans in the planning process
- is creative
- considers long-term goals while also working towards short-term objectives
- is aligned with the company's values, culture and purpose
- produces results.

Doesn't this sound like the sort of planning that individuals could benefit from?

Unfortunately, most of the personal planning people do lacks many of these attributes. Often it lacks structure – people usually call it "having a think about things". It tends to focus on short-term problems, such as difficulties in a relationship; or on specific opportunities, such as buying a house or a career opportunity.

When we plan in this way we are often reacting to external forces or changes, rather than operating out of our long-term goals. This type of planning is generally *re*active rather than *pro*active, and because it lacks structure, it often leads us to make expedient decisions which we may later regret.

Alternatively, our unstructured planning may be "daydreaming". Unfortunately, daydreaming is totally ungrounded in our current situation and ignores the reality around us. This type of planning generally leads us nowhere. Nothing comes of it.

In our unstructured planning, we rarely write our thoughts and ideas down on paper and so we miss the opportunity to consider all the facts and to brainstorm all the possible solutions. Instead we can fall into the trap of choosing the most obvious solutions, those solutions which first come to mind.

Most people's "thinking about things" also lacks another important factor – *creativity*. We drop into "thought patterns" – well-worn ways of thinking about our lives. Very little energy is directed towards innovative ideas. It's no wonder we then don't want to act on our plans. We are bored with them before we start.

So how do we avoid these common pitfalls? How do we achieve the kind of planning in our personal lives that organizations strive for – the planning that leads to success?

First we must move from "thinking about things" to "thinking about our thinking". Let's start to do that now.

Research on human decision-making and problem-solving indicates that, broadly speaking, there are two types of thinking – right-brain thinking and left-brain thinking.

Left-brain thinking follows a logical pattern. It is objective rather than subjective and considers things as either true or false, black or white. Left-brain thinking is logical, rational and structured. Left-brain answers to the question, "What uses can you think of for a brick?" would include building a house or a wall.

Conversely, the type of thinking that generates creative solutions is *right-brain thinking*. Right-brain thinking follows intuitive hunches and creates patterns, often without following a step-by-step process. Solutions generated by right-brain thinking may initially not appear logical or sensible, but they are often creative. Right-brain answers to the uses for a brick question may include using it as a doorstop or breaking it in half to make two bookends.

Most of us have a tendency to use one side of the brain more than the other. This can limit our ability to resolve issues and find solutions. Important opportunities can be missed because we are locked into using only one type of thinking. And at either extreme, an idea may be highly creative but not practical, or it may be extremely rational but completely uninspiring.

Successful personal planning requires thinking which comes from both sides of the brain, thinking which is both structured and creative – thinking that is grounded in reality but is also innovative and inspiring.

Let's face it: we are all more likely to commit to plans if they are creative and inspire us. The most effective leaders have always known that people must be inspired to follow them – not convinced through rational arguments.

So our personal planning needs to be both structured and creative, but what other attributes should our planning have?

Effective planning must build *personal ownership*. Personal ownership means we personally *"own the plan"*. We are committed to the plan and want to follow it through, to make it happen. And how do we build this personal ownership? By bringing our own content to the planning and by designing the plan ourselves.

The personal strategic planning method in this chapter achieves this objective. *Your* personal strategic plan is built on the dimensions of your life that you define – *your* key content areas – and the purpose you define for each of these dimensions – *your* statements of purpose.

Because your key content areas and statements of purpose have been built on the foundations of your personal values, your personal planning will be *aligned* with your personal values. This is vital. Otherwise your personal strategic planning does not reflect who you really are. It is not grounded in reality.

The personal strategic planning method also takes a long-term perspective. It starts with your long-term goals and works logically back through shorter and shorter time periods. In doing this you develop specific outcomes with a number of different time horizons.

This method has a proven track record. It has worked effectively in a large number of organizations and for many individuals. *Used regularly it will change your life*. We personally use it and it has changed our lives in deep and fundamental ways.

THE PERSONAL STRATEGIC PLANNING METHOD

In chapter 9, the life circle activity provided a way to create a picture of the present, represented as your current key content areas and your statements of purpose. Planning involves creating a vision or a picture of the future. Now we will use your key content areas and statements of purpose again to do just that.

Let's start by thinking many years into the future. Think about yourself in, say, ten or twenty years from now. Select a time horizon that makes sense for you. If you are currently working in paid employment, maybe you could select a time a few years before you are thinking of retiring. If you have children you may select a time just before or just after you anticipate they might leave home.

The first step is to imagine what your life will look like at that time. Take each of your key content areas in turn and think about the following questions:

- Will I still have this same key content area? Or, might it have merged with another, or disappeared entirely?
- Would any new key content areas have emerged? What might they be? How would I define them?
- What would be the key relationships in my life in twenty years from now?
- What changes in society, technology or the environment may have occurred during that time? How would these affect my key content areas?

Now, draw your life circle for that time in the future. This will include any new key content areas you might have developed, and exclude any current key content areas you think will no longer exist. Once you have developed your new life circle, consider the following questions for each of your future key content areas:

- What do I want to have achieved in this key content area in twenty years' time?
- What skills do I want to have twenty years from now?
- What personal experiences and activities do I want to have achieved?
- What would be the tangible demonstration or display of my achievements?
- What would be the important achievements in terms of those key relationships?
- What would I consider success to be?

You may also wish to come up with some other creative questions which are relevant for you to ask yourself.

Write some words or a few sentences to answer these questions for each one of your key content areas. Remember that you are thinking many years, maybe twenty years or so, into the future, so don't think too small. You may not have even started working towards some of these achievements. For example, your goal may be to send your children to college, run your own company or take care of an elderly partner or parent. Remember to think about your success in terms of the key relationships in your life. What will these important relationships look like in twenty years from now?

The process you have just gone through has been the beginning of the development of your long-term strategic plan. This plan will be in the form of a series of phrases or sentences describing your hopes, dreams and aspirations for your life. Don't worry if some of these seem a bit vague or unrealistic, or if you are not sure how you will get there. They are your long-term vision. They may seem somewhat unrealistic at the moment.

Often when people complete their plans they seem surprised that the process is not as mysterious as they had expected. You may also feel the same way. But do not forget the foundation work you have put into getting here. In the preceding chapters you developed your personal journey timeline, your values pyramid, your key content areas, your life circle and your statements of purpose. A good deal of work went into this and this has provided the bedrock on which to build your personal strategic plan.

Now with your long-term personal strategic plan established, you can select a medium-term time horizon and repeat the process. This will help establish how you will get there and what may happen along the way.

FIVE-YEAR PLANS

Let's now develop a medium-term personal strategic plan, say five years out. Begin again by considering whether the same key content areas for your life currently could apply in five years' time. If necessary, revise your life circle. Again, thinking about each key content area consider these questions:

- What do I want to have achieved in this key content area in five years' time?
- What skills do I want to have in five years from now?
- What personal experiences and activities do I want to have achieved?
- What would be the tangible demonstration or display of my achievements?
- What would be the important achievements in terms of those key relationships?
- What would I consider success to be?

For your five-year plan, write some words or a few sentences to describe your answers to these types of questions for each key content area.

Don't forget to review how well your five-year plan fits within your twenty-year plan. After all, you complete your five-year plan on your way to your twenty-year plan. Do they fit together well? Should you revise any details? If necessary, adjust your twenty-year plan by referring to your five-year plan and vice versa. As much as possible, your personal strategic plans for different time-frames should be in alignment, like a series of personal signposts leading into the future.

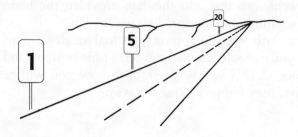

ONE-YEAR PLANS

Finally, let's look over the next twelve months – one year out. Look at each of your current key content areas in your life circle. Consider the following questions:

- Are any of your key content areas likely to change?
- What do you want to achieve in each key content area?

Now work through the same questions you considered for your five-year and twenty-year key content areas. Again, just a few sentences or phrases will do.

Your answers for your one-year plan should be more tangible than your five-year and twenty-year answers. You should be able clearly to identify your desired achievements at the end of the year. You should be able to imagine what things might look like at that time. You should be able to point to each one and say, "I have done that" or "I have not done that."

This one-year plan comprises your personal *New Year's resolutions* for the coming year. And this one-year plan should start you on the road to achieving your five- and twenty-year goals. Your short-term resolutions are therefore embedded in your medium- and long-term goals. Everything should now be in alignment because you have started with the longest time period and worked back to the present.

In effect, you have created a set of "stacked" life circles, developing from the present out into the future years towards your long-term personal vision. You could, in fact, draw a life circle for every year of your life in the future. If you did, you could imagine it looking something like this.

Now you have designed your personal strategic plan you can use it in creative ways. A few suggestions are:

- Add your twenty-, five- and one-year resolutions to your life circle and take it with you to work every day... or stick it on the wall or refrigerator at home.
- Give your key content areas names which mean something to you. Name some of your key content areas after animals, places, famous people, pieces of music, ice-cream flavors, anything that is meaningful to you.

Remember, it can be *a lack of creativity* that underlies the lack of soul in our lives. We lack the creative spark to find soul. Remember that your personal strategic plan needs to be creative and inspire you personally.

Finally, all strategic plans should be living works. They should be viewed and reviewed, updated and revised, pondered, and occasionally torn to shreds and begun again from scratch.

Also, consider your personal strategic plan a road map to the main highway – but that doesn't mean you can't occasionally wander down an interesting side-road or two. Opportunities arise that you have not anticipated – for example, someone makes you an offer you shouldn't refuse – or sometimes you will achieve goals faster than you expected. After all, we know that both order and chaos are a part of life.

CHAPTER TWELVE

MAKING BETTER CHOICES, BUILDING BETTER HABITS

P ERSONAL SUCCESS invariably requires personal change. To achieve personal change – to move from our current position to where we want to be – requires *action*. All the personal planning in the world is of very limited value unless it translates into concrete action. Turning plans into action is where "the rubber hits the road", so to speak. So far, we have focused on personal planning; now let us shift the focus onto how to turn your personal strategic plan into reality.

Between the idea
And the reality
Between the motion
And the act
Falls the Shadow

from "The Hollow Men",
T. S. Eliot

Our personal actions and our success are largely determined by *our personal choices and habits*. For example, Michelangelo's choices of composition and color, combined with his habits of hard work and persever-ance, made the painting of the Sistine Chapel a great success.

Choices are individual decisions. Deciding which car to buy, whether to take a job offer, what to have for lunch – these are all examples of choices.

Habits, on the other hand, are patterns of behavior or actions. Working hard, smoking, regular exercise are all examples of habits. Another way to describe a habit is a group of similar choices. When we choose to buy the news-paper every morning on the way to work – that choice, once firmly established, becomes a habit.

In his book *The Seven Habits of Highly Effective People*, Dr Stephen Covey says that habits are found at the "intersection of knowledge, skill and desire" and that to create a habit we must work on all three of these dimensions.

Habits are certainly important in achieving personal success. However, by themselves, they are not enough. Making decisions like when to resign and take a new job, or how to invest your retirement savings are not habits, they are individual choices. These individual choices can have a profound effect on the direction our lives take.

In the mid-1980s, while Nancy worked as a money-market dealer, she invested heavily in the stock market. She borrowed from her retirement funds and, with the help of her broker, developed a portfolio of stocks which included blue-chip companies, high-tech firms, financial institutions, some overseas companies and resources-based firms.

Nancy really enjoyed investing in the financial market and would closely monitor her shares on the computer screens at work. Her investments performed nicely, showing strong growth in every quarter through 1985 and 1986.

Nancy reviewed the situation closely early in 1987 and calculated that her original investment had doubled in value. She could therefore withdraw her original investment from the stock market and purchase a rental property, while leaving the remaining funds in the stock market. As the market seemed set for a correction, Nancy decided this would be the best decision. While share prices kept climbing, Nancy reduced her exposure and by the middle of the year had withdrawn sufficient funds to purchase her rental property.

Nancy watched in horror the day the stock market crashed in October, wiping out 80 per cent of the value of her remaining shares in just one day. Her profits simply disappeared before her eyes as the cursor on the computer screen updated the share prices. She tried desperately to phone her broker to find out what to do, but his telephone was constantly engaged. Many of her friends had also invested heavily in the stock market and had lost their entire savings.

By the end of the day, Nancy was a nervous wreck. "All that work studying the stock market wasted," she thought. "At least I got my initial investment out." Two weeks later Nancy purchased her investment property.

While Nancy's habits of regularly studying the share prices, seeking professional advice and sticking to her strategy were important, they did not protect her from potential disaster. After all, many of her friends had had similar habits and they had lost all their money. It was Nancy's single choice to reduce her exposure to the stock market at that time that had protected her retirement savings.

Finding soul also requires making better choices and better habits. Soul, for all its mystery, has to do with how and what we think, and what we feel, do and experience. Because soul is concerned with personal meaning, our individual choices and personal habits can either help or hinder us in building personal meaning. So, rather than waiting for a bolt of lightning or some mystical experience, it is better to adopt an active approach to building meaning in our lives.

We don't stand around waiting for success to happen to us. Why should we expect soul to be any different?

In India, Sadhus, or holy men, spend many hours a day meditating. They are not sitting there waiting for a spiritual experience. Their meditation is an active habit and soul is found in their practice, not in "waiting" and hoping that if they sit there long enough it will strike them.

Disappointed? Not very mysterious? Sounds too easy? Well, it can be easy if we realize it is about doing things we have always done – making decisions and building habits – it is just about learning to do them better.

So let's start by looking at our personal choices.

We make a choice when we decide between two or more alternatives, and the process of making a choice is commonly called *decision-making*. Decision-making typically occurs as a reaction to a problem or opportunity, or when we experience a difference between the current situation and what is desired. While decision-making can involve groups or organizations, here we will focus on individual decision-making.

If we wish to make better choices we must improve the quality of our decision-making. In order to improve the quality of our decision-making, we must first understand how we make decisions.

We all make decisions in different ways, using different methods of decision-making at different times. Our decision-making is dependent on personal factors, such as our values, skills, experience and motivation, as well as environmental factors, such as the type of decision we are making and the surroundings in which we make our decisions.

Ricardo is a computer systems analyst. Two valuable skills for a systems analyst are solving problems and making decisions. Ricardo is excellent at both, particularly when there is a tight time-frame and a quick decision is required. Set him a problem like, "Our computer network isn't working. What can be done to fix it?" and the first thing he will ask is, "How long do I have to work out the problem?"

It is always a pleasure to watch Ricardo go about his work. If you give him half an hour he uses it in the most efficient way possible; 10 minutes trying to understand what the problem is, followed by 15 minutes finding possible solutions, and finally 5 minutes summarizing the pros and cons of each solution and giving his recommendation.

Why is Ricardo's problem-solving so effective? First, he allocates enough time to analyze and understand the problem. Then he carefully collects all the available data and looks not just for the "best" solution, but for a range of possible solutions. Even if he feels that he has found the best solution in the first five minutes he continues to look for other solutions that might exist. Finally, he summarizes all the potential options and looks at which is the best solution. The key to his effectiveness is that he uses a structured approach to decision-making.

Contrast Ricardo's decision-making process with that used on a TV game show. In the concluding segment of the show, Betty, this week's "successful contestant", must put nine household items in order from least expensive to most expensive.

This relatively simple task is made rather difficult by a number of factors: the studio audience yelling "advice" to her, the short time-frame provided to make the necessary decisions, and Betty's own stress level, created by her concern to take advantage of this "once-in-a-lifetime opportunity". This is a sub-optimal environment for effective decision-making – it is little wonder that she ends up with the wrong answer.

The differences between Ricardo's and Betty's decision-making processes are striking and just go to show how this process can vary significantly from person to person and situation to situation.

Everyday Decision-Making

Although making decisions is central to most people's lives, we seldom think about the decision-making *process* itself. Consequently, our decision-making often suffers from a range of problems.

We rarely take into account all of the relevant thoughts, feelings and experiences as we ponder a range of potential choices. If we are particularly emotional, for example, our emotions may cloud our decision-making, causing us to delay decisions, act impulsively or collect information obsessively.

Time can also be an important factor, especially if there is insufficient time to make a well-reasoned choice. Believing there isn't enough time to search for options and think them through may lead to what psychologists call a state of *hypervigilance* – a frantic search for information or alternatives that is both stressful and not well thought through.

Mentally, we have a limited ability to process a multitude of facts and often we don't consider all the possible alternatives. Sometimes alternatives may not be seen or all consequences of our decisions are not considered. On some occasions information may not be accurate, or even known. In addition, we may be slow to learn and consequently repeat the same mistakes over and over.

Also, decisions are made when there is a difference between the current situation and what is desired. In this situation we often find ourselves in a heightened state of activity or stress which can also undermine our decision-making.

We may practice defensive avoidance, procrastinating and making excuses like "There isn't anything better around anyway..." or "It doesn't matter if I don't decide until next week..." On the other hand, sometimes we go to the opposite extreme – we rush in and make decisions without sufficient thought.

We do give *reasons* why we make decisions, but these reasons are often justifications *after* the decision-making process is complete. Sometimes we may blame others for our decisions, particularly if we are unhappy with the outcome. Or we may say we had no choice, when actually we did exercise our choice.

In summary then, there are many shortcomings in our everyday decision-making processes.

The need for personal control

In addition to the skills we have and the situation we find ourselves in, personal decision-making is also strongly influenced by the desire or need for personal control. The desire for personal control, which is a personality trait, is the extent to which a person is generally motivated to see themselves in control of the events in their lives.

People vary in their desire to be in control or feel in control of their lives. Some of us have a low desire for control, while others have an extremely high desire for control.

> Jessica runs a large department in a major corporation. She has control over a multimillion-dollar budget and two hundred staff. As if this wasn't enough, she regularly gets involved in issues at work outside her direct area of influence. By her own admission she has a high desire for control. If there is a meeting, she wants to run it. If she and her partner are having a dinner party, she has to be the one to organize it. A relative of hers passed away recently. She made it clear to everyone that she would be the one who would arrange the funeral. Jessica enjoys controlling the world around her. In fact the thing she says she loves most about her job is that she gets to make decisions. She is clear in her own mind that control and decision-making are closely related and she seeks and enjoys both.

Our desire for control is also dependent on our environment. We all experience situations where we would prefer to exercise a great deal of control and, conversely, situations where we are happy to have little or no control. For example, some senior executives who are very control-oriented at work are happy to let their partners or families run everything outside the office. However, we all exhibit a *general* level of desire for personal control.

So what does our need for control have to do with personal success and decision-making?

Research indicates that the need for control correlates with the need for achievement. People who desire a high degree of control have been found to aspire to higher levels of achievement, while people who have a low desire for control have been found to aspire to lower levels of achievement.

Those people with a high need for control have also been found to respond to challenges with more effort, and to persist longer to solve them. People who have a low desire for control sometimes let something or someone else define what success means to them.

So, understanding your own need for control is important. While there is a range of psychological tests which can measure your need for control, you can probably get some idea of your need for control by thinking about the following questions.

Do I prefer ...
... a job where I have a lot of control over what I do and when?
... to be a leader rather than a follower?
... to avoid situations where someone else tells me what to do?
Or do I ...
... prefer someone else to take over the leadership role when I am involved in a group project?
... tend to push many of life's decisions off onto someone else?
... prefer to wait and see if someone else is going to solve a problem so that I don't have to be bothered with it?
... tend to think others know better what is best for me?

If you tend to agree with the first few statements it is more likely that you are someone with a high need for control. If you agree more with the last few statements then you are more likely to be someone for whom control is less important.

Remember though, just because you have a low desire for control does not mean you are unable to take more control of your decisions. It simply means that you don't *need* it or tend to *seek* it. In some ways, you can count your blessings that you are not *driven* in the way that people with a high need for control can be driven.

Finally, because values form the basis of much of what a person does, values play an important role in decision-making. This is why we have spent so much time on values in this book. *Being clear about our values is one of the cornerstones of effective and potent decision-making.*

DECISION-MAKING EXAMINED

Social psychologists Irving Janis and Leon Mann have conducted extensive research on personal decision-making. They have identified a number of important characteristics of effective decision-making. We have drawn on their research here, while adding many of our own thoughts and observations. In addition, at the end of this section on effective decision-making, we have included a useful "decision-making checklist" which you may find helpful when you are making a decision.

EFFECTIVE DECISION-MAKING

Effective decision-making involves a number of stages. First, there must be a *willingness to make a choice* and some level of *comprehension* of the problem. Secondly, *information* for decision-making is required and from this information a number of choices need to be formulated. Before selecting a choice, the *consequences* of each choice need to be determined and these consequences assessed relative to issues like ethics. Once we have made a choice, *commitment to action* is then required. And finally, we need to *live with our decision*.

To make effective decisions, we also need to bring a number of other attributes into the process. All effective decision-making needs to consider *emotions*. In fact, it could be argued that all important decisions involve emotion. If no emotion is involved, it is probably not a very important decision.

Effective decision-making involves *risk*. The willingness to take risks and to consider risky choices increases our ability to make effective decisions.

Creativity increases the effectiveness of our decision-making in many ways – in defining the problem, brainstorming choices, making a choice and implementing that choice.

Finally, being willing to apply our *individuality* to our decisions increases the effectiveness of our decision-making – for example, being willing to define our own problems and make our own choices.

These are the attributes of effective decision-making. Let's now consider this process in more detail.

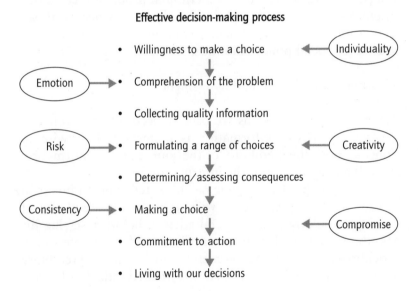

Effective decision-making process

Willingness and comprehension

A number of important prerequisites are essential for effective decision-making. Initially, there must be a willingness to make a *choice*. Many people get caught up at this early stage of decision-making. It is like standing at a fork in the road and being unable to decide which direction to take

– sometimes we even turn back the way we came. How often do we hear people say, in the face of options, "I *just* can't decide"? Sometimes the very number and diversity of options that face us lead to the inability to make a choice. Embarking on the decision-making process seems too difficult. Nonetheless, willingness to make a choice is a necessary first step.

Next, we must have some *comprehension* of the problem or opportunity with which we are faced. Being able clearly to define the problem or opportunity is vital, because it establishes the context in which we search for alternatives. As is often said, "Knowing the right questions to ask is just as important as knowing the answers." For example, defining the issue of illicit drug use as a criminal problem focuses our attention on criminal and legal solutions, whereas if we define this problem as a social issue we are more likely to search for social policy solutions.

Information gathering and assessment

When we make decisions we usually need information, and the quality of this information is important. It is wise to consider both the credibility of the source of the information as well as the quality of the information itself.

For example, if Fred your neighbor tells you to invest in XYZ Company it would be wise to assess the credibility of Fred, particularly as a financial advisor, before assessing his specific recommendation. After all, if Fred is a professional stockbroker then his recommendation has more credibility than if he works in a completely unrelated industry. Even if the source of information appears sound, it would be worthwhile understanding how Fred arrived at his specific recommendation.

Formulation of choices

Having gathered information, we then need to formulate a *range of choices*. These choices may be developed using a number of different techniques, for example:

- spending some time thinking about it
- making a list
- brainstorming with others
- thinking about how you have resolved this issue or similar issues in the past
- calling on the expertise or experience of others, or perhaps
- finding out how someone you respect or admire solved the problem in their own lives.

When faced with a decision, it is useful to remember we really only ever have three options: we can change the situation we find ourselves in; we can accept the situation and decide to adapt to it; or we can leave the situation.

Let's look at an example. Say you are in a job you dislike. The option you would probably most often think of is leaving. Just find another job. The other option may be to speak to your manager and express your desire for some change. By changing the situation, you may be happier with it.

> We only ever have three choices:
> - change the situation
> - accept the situation
> - leave the situation.

However, sometimes we don't have the option to change the situation or to leave it. We shouldn't forget that, sometimes, acceptance is a very real option. This is not necessarily "copping out" or giving up. Sometimes it is the smart option. In some job situations, biding our time may be the best decision in the short term (or even in the longer term). Although acceptance seems like the "do nothing" option, the very act of acceptance can change the way we see a situation and helps us to cope with it. Also, when we decide to accept a situation, we can then come up with strategies to cope while we need to live with it.

Consequences

Having formulated a range of choices, the *consequences* of each of these choices need to be determined and evaluated. All decisions that are acted upon have consequences.

Understanding the potential consequences of our actions is an important part of assessing choices.

To assess the consequences of our actions we must think about the effects of our actions:

- What are the likely impacts of the decision?
- Will the decision achieve the desired outcome or outcomes?
- What other outcomes are possible?
- Are we happy with these potential impacts?

These are not always easy questions to answer. When we think through the potential consequences of our actions we cannot always predict all possible outcomes. Chaos and complexity preclude a simple direct link between cause and effect, action and reaction. However, this does not totally negate the value of assessing the likely impacts of our decisions.

When we look at the consequences of our decisions we often identify potential impacts on other people or the world around us. This raises an important ethical question: *How can we tell what is a good decision and what is a bad decision?*

A Chinese proverb

One day a man woke up to find that the horse he had recently purchased had run away. His neighbor came over and offered words of commiseration. The man replied, "Who knows what is good and what is bad?"

The next day the horse returned with a group of wild horses it had gathered together. The neighbor came across and offered words of congratulations at his good fortune at having gained so many horses. The man answered, "How do we know what is good and what is bad?"

The next day the man's son decided to ride one of the new horses. He fell off the horse and broke his leg. The neighbor came across and offered words of commiseration. The man answered, "How can we know what is good and what is bad?"

The next day the army came to visit, recruiting men for the war; but they did not take the man's son because he had a broken leg.

The neighbor came across and offered his congratulations. And again the man said, "How can it be known what is good and what is bad?"

This story from Chinese folklore illustrates how we can never be quite sure whether a decision is good or a bad. The Yin and Yang – the intertwining of opposites – of the good and the bad also represent this way of looking at the world. The two are intertwined rather than sharply divided into opposites. It is the same with decision-making. What is a good decision and what is a bad decision? Often it is not that easy to tell.

As a guide to making a good decision, we can listen to our conscience. This ethical guide is our inner voice which informs us of the intentions of our actions. You can use the following questions to tap into your conscience:

> The moral quality of an action is always determined by the intention of the actor.
>
> *Indian saying*

- Who is either directly or indirectly affected by my decision? (If you wish, make a list of these stakeholders in your decision.)
- What are the likely impacts of my decision on these stakeholders?
- Should I consult any of these stakeholders?
- If someone did the same thing to me, what would I think of them?
- If it happened to someone I care about, what would I think?
- If all my friends and colleagues knew about my decision, what would they think?

Making a choice

Once we have assessed the potential consequences of the various choices, we need to determine the strengths and weaknesses of each choice. This helps bring the decision-making process to a resolution. A "logical", rational approach is not the only valid one for making a choice. While usually considered a "poor cousin" to the logico-rational approach, *intuition* can guide the process of making a choice. How often have we made a rational choice only to realize later that the correct decision would have been the one our intuition told us to choose? We hear people say, "I should have gone with my gut feeling."

This point in decision-making is often the most stressful. Perhaps this is because we realize how significant making a choice is. When we make a choice, we change the direction of our lives. We also sometimes close off other options, potentially forever. We often hear people say, "I just want to keep my options open." Sometimes we would rather live in the "limbo" of possibility than take the step towards a single choice.

Commitment

Commitment is one of the most important aspects of good decision-making. Commitment is the act of following through on decisions that we have made. It is a shame to mention commitment simply as if it were a *fait accompli* – as we all know, following through is often the most difficult part.

> Mark has a part-time job selling vinyl siding by phone. His job is to ring potential customers to arrange a meeting between the customer and one of the company's on-the-road sales representatives. The company is fortunate that Mark is an expert at convincing customers of the many benefits of vinyl siding – its durability, low maintenance and cost effectiveness. Mark's natural charm and sales skills regularly convince customers to commit rather easily to a visit from one of the salespeople.
>
> Unfortunately for the sales reps, customers don't always follow through their commitment to a sales visit. Many get someone else to call back and say they are out of town or they hide behind their curtains when the rep comes around and don't answer the door. While they are happy to commit over the phone when speaking to someone charming and engaging, their resolve disappears when they see they might end up being convinced to actually buy something.

Unfortunately, in our society it has become the rule to commit rather easily to things. People make promises quickly and easily, and break them just as quickly. Often, however, we are simply committing to *starting* something rather than to seeing it through. Similarly, we may be committed to an idea rather than to a specific action.

People with a strong sense of personal direction rarely commit to things they don't follow through.

We can take steps to ensure that when we say we are going to commit we really are going to commit. Some steps that can help are:

- Don't answer or decide straight away. Give yourself time, or ask for time, to consider whether you really want to pursue something and whether you have the time.
- If you like, commit to a short "trial" period of time and see how it goes before committing long term.
- When you are asked to commit to something, check to see if it fits in with your personal values, statements of purpose and your personal strategic plans.
- Be prepared to say "no".

A person's word sometimes doesn't seem to mean much nowadays; we expect to be able to change our minds at the drop of a hat and to un-commit as quickly as we commit. This is not the foundation of effective decision-making, nor is it likely to improve our relationships with other people, so take making a commitment seriously and make your word count.

Living with our decisions

In George Orwell's famous book *1984*, the dictatorial government of Oceania has an entire department dedicated to rewriting history. The Ministry of Truth employs thousands of people whose primary role is to "update" old news stories and publications.

By rewriting history the government of Oceania could control what was learned from the past. Changing the past was not just about controlling the government's current image, it was a deliberate effort to control the future.

The past can hold lessons and answers. Honoring and accepting the past is an important part of effective decision-making. It is one of the first important steps towards creating the future.

Unlike the government in George Orwell's *1984*, we cannot rewrite history, especially our own history; we must live with it and try to accept it without guilt or defensiveness. We must live with our decisions and the consequences of our actions.

In living with the past the concept of *absolution* can be helpful. Literally, absolution means to be released from guilt or punishment. Absolution allows us to leave the past behind and move on.

The practice of absolution is common among many religions. In the Catholic Church, for example, the priest acts as God's representative to absolve sins. Most methods of absolution, such as saying prayers, burning notes, washing the body or ringing bells, are ritualistic and symbolic.

If you have trouble leaving the past behind and moving on, you may wish to develop your own absolution ritual to absolve yourself. Here are some ideas, but basically whatever works for you is fine:

- make up a small saying
- write a journal or diary entry
- create a personal journey timeline that captures the decision
- buy or sell something that carries a symbolic meaning.

In addition to the process of effective decision-making, we need to bring *six important attributes* into our decision-making – emotions, creativity, individuality, risk-taking, consistency and compromise.

Emotions

A few years ago a large resource company was looking to sell off one of its divisions. It was a very important decision and the senior executives discussed it a great deal. The division to be sold owned one of the first mines ever opened by the company. For many people there was considerable heritage attached to this mine. The mine was part of the company's corporate history.

Before making a final decision, some of the executives, including the company president, went to the mine site to review the operation. As they got into a car at the airport, the president directed the driver to a particular street on the way to the mine's site office. When they were in the street, he asked the driver to stop in front of a particular house. He pointed to the house and said to the other company executives, "See that house, that's where I grew up."

The other executives then knew that this was an important and difficult decision for the president and they recognized the amount of emotional attachment involved.

It has been argued that no important decision is ever made without some *emotional involvement*. For example, purchasing a house or condominium in which you plan to live is an emotional decision – after all, it will be your home, as well as possibly being one of the most important investment decisions you make.

Decisions we make which do not include an emotional component are often unimportant or less important decisions. For example, if someone asks whether you want tea or coffee, milk or cream, it is not likely to be an emotional decision (unless you're dieting!).

> Choice is not just about actions, it's also about how you react or feel about something.

Advertisers understand the importance of the emotional factors in decision-making. They need to, because advertising is about influencing the decisions we make. Successful advertisers often use emotional appeals to convince us to make a purchasing decision. For example, they may link feelings of confidence, power and excitement with a new car, or feelings of love and care with washing powder for clothes.

Some of the emotions connected with decision-making are fear, anger, depression, happiness, joy, disappointment and guilt. Often a number of emotions can coexist, particularly when there are advantages and disadvantages with a range of choices.

For these reasons, consideration of emotional factors should be an integral part of all important decisions. Ignoring emotional factors could, in fact, lead to a poor decision.

Creativity

Creativity can be used at two stages of the decision-making process. First, we can think creatively when we define a problem or opportunity. For example, rather than define a job loss as a career problem, we could define it as an opportunity to do further study. Secondly, we can think creatively when we generate different choices. For example, rather than do an MBA, we could choose to study history because companies are becoming interested in capturing their corporate histories.

Various techniques can help us introduce creativity to our decision-making. One of the most useful is *mind mapping*.

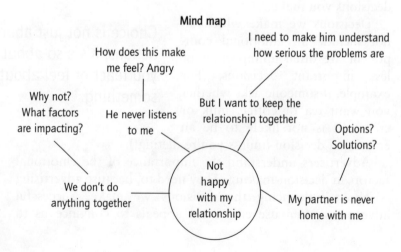

Mind map

In this technique we start with the central issue and, following our thought-flow, build out from it. Related ideas are joined together by a line and separate ideas build out along a different stem. This technique can help us get all our thoughts and feelings out in a visual form.

Individuality

Individuality is an important factor in effective decision-making. English philosopher John Stuart Mill wrote on individuality and decision-making in the 1800s. This is what he said:

> He who lets the world, or his own portion of it, choose his plan of life for him, has no need for any other faculty than the ape-like one of imitation. He who chooses his plan for himself, employs all his faculties. He must use observation to see, reasoning and judgement to foresee, activity to gather materials for decision, discrimination to decide, and when he has decided, firmness and self-control to hold to his deliberate decision... The human faculties of perception, judgement, discriminative feeling, mental activity, and even moral preference, are exercised only in making a choice. He who does anything because it is the custom, makes no choice.

Although John Stuart Mill was writing over 100 years ago, his words speak directly to us today. We do have a great many choices to make, probably far more than in Mill's time. But how often do we truly express our individuality in our decision-making by making a choice, rather than simply selecting from a range of "acceptable" or usual options?

As we have discussed previously, the pressure to conform to social norms can be substantial. When we accept these social norms, we also accept the values that accompany them. These values may not reflect our own personal values. In addition, our choices may not be in line with our life's purpose and personal strategic plans. This results in poor decision-making.

The more you express your individuality, the more human you become.

It can be argued that when we follow the "pack" or accept "the right way to do things", we are not really making a decision; and if we are following others, we have no need for effective decision-making skills at all.

Alternatively, we may exercise choice in areas where it really doesn't matter. For example, a question put to us recently was, "Do you want wet froth or dry froth on your cappuccino?" These niceties of customer service sometimes present us with unimportant choices to make.

However, when we make *real and important* choices we need to exercise our judgment, discrimination, self-control, commitment and resolve. If we believe these personal attributes are worth nurturing, we must strive to express our individuality – it is fundamental to our well-being, to our long-term happiness and to finding soul in our lives. We can do this by being aware of the degree of individuality expressed in our choices when we are making decisions.

Risk-taking

At different ages we are more willing to *take risks*. Children often learn by taking risks; by experimentation they define boundaries and limits. As we grow older, however, we often become less willing to take risks. It seems as though the more of life we see, the more we worry about the potential risks of our decisions. Often we feel we have more to lose than gain from risk-taking. Unfortunately, not taking risks can have serious implications.

Bob works for a financial institution in a middle-management role. He is forty-nine years old and has been with the company for twenty-six years. Bob is intelligent and was a rising star with the company early in his career; in fact, he was the youngest departmental manager in the company.

After he had been there for ten years, the company was restructured and Bob's department was decentralized from head office to a smaller service unit. Out of the head office limelight, Bob's career soon stalled and he began to feel the company had let him down. He considered leaving and starting his own business, but with two young children he was concerned about the potential risk to his retirement savings.

Bob decided to wait. "Maybe the company will change its mind," he thought. "I might be lucky; there might be another restructure. Anyway, other opportunities are sure to come along."

Sixteen years later, Bob is in the same job and further restructuring has caused many of his original staff to move on. Now his savings with the company retirement scheme are even more substantial and, although his children have grown up, the desire to start his own business has gone.

Not surprisingly, Bob feels the company, which he has been so loyal to, has let him down. He lacks motivation and often rings in sick with one of many on-going health problems. Somewhere along the line, Bob's fire went out.

What is the personal cost of these actions? Apart from the health impacts, there is an *opportunity cost*. Opportunity cost is a concept used in finance when comparing different investment options. It means that if I make a decision to put my money in one type of investment, I am also making a decision to miss out on, or forgo, other types of investment. For example, if I buy a house today, I am forgoing other investment opportunities such as buying shares or a business. An opportunity is lost and this comes at some cost.

It's the same with decisions we make about how we invest our time and energy. If we invest our time and energy in one thing, it is not available for doing something else. This is what Bob is doing. He has invested his time in a job he no longer has a passion for – that's a very poor investment. He not only gets a poor return from the job he is doing, but he also misses an opportunity to do something he could have had a better return on.

There is often an opportunity cost in decision-making and risk-taking. Like Bob, sometimes when we decide not to take a risk it can cost us *twice*, not just once.

Taking risks is about purpose and commitment.

When our decisions and actions are directed towards our life's purpose and what is meaningful to us, risk-taking is put into context. Our risks are directed towards what we believe is important, not simply towards taking advantage of a lucky break or opportunity, or just for the sake of it.

Consistency

Consistency is also necessary for effective decision-making. Consistency refers to the stability and reliability of our decision-making. Erratic decision-making rarely serves us well and will, over time, reduce our achievements. As an example, in our family, budgeting has never been our strong point. In the early days in particular, we would make a big decision to save for something, but then when it was done we would fall back into old habits. After a while we would realize that "the wheels had fallen off" our financial planning, so we would make another big decision to take more control. The inconsistency in our decision-making has significantly reduced our effectiveness in this area of our lives.

Consistency in decision-making is also important because it helps build habits. What else is a habit but doing something consistently?

Compromise

Effective decision-making often involves *compromise*. A compromise occurs when practical realities require unobtainable ideals to be modified, or when our wishes and desires clash with those of someone else who will be affected by our decision.

The ability to compromise can be a sign of maturity. Improving the quality of our relationships often requires compromise.

Here we have provided a decision-making checklist to help you pull together these ideas on effective decision-making. You may find it useful to refer to this checklist when you are making important choices.

YOUR PERSONAL DECISION-MAKING CHECKLIST

Opportunity or problem definition
- Can I clearly state what the opportunity or problem is? (Try writing it in one sentence.)

Choice identification
- Do I have a choice?
- Have I allowed sufficient time to consider my choices?
- What are the emotional aspects of the opportunity or problem?
- What choices do I have?
- Have I thought creatively about my options?
- What would someone I admire or respect do in the same situation?
- Should I seek the advice of a friend or expert in the area?

Choice assessment
- What is the quality of the information I am using to make my decision?
- Which choices improve the quality of my relationships with others? Which choices improve the quality of my relationship with the environment?
- How am I expressing my individuality in each choice?

- What is the opportunity cost of each option? What other options will I eliminate by this decision?
- Am I happy about the amount of personal control I will have with each option?
- What is the quality of my sources of information?
- Which of the alternatives is consistent with my personal values, life's purpose and personal strategic plan?

Ethical assessment

- Who is either directly or indirectly affected by my decision? (If you wish, make a list of the stakeholders in your decision.)
- What are the likely impacts of my decision on these stakeholders?
- Should I consult any of these stakeholders?
- If someone did the same thing to me, what would I think of them?
- If it happened to someone I care about, what would I think?
- If all my friends and colleagues knew about my decision, what would they think?

Choice selection and commitment

- What are the overall advantages and disadvantages of each choice?
- Can choices be combined to find a better solution?
- What choice or choices am I willing to commit to?
- Have I identified all the risks associated with committing to this choice?
- Am I willing to commit to these risks?
- Am I emotionally committed to this choice?
- What is the best timing for this decision? When do I need to commit?

BUILDING BETTER HABITS

Once you are making effective decisions you are well on the way to building better habits. After all, a habit is a pattern of decisions or ongoing commitment to a decision, and habits, just like effective decision-making, require discipline and personal commitment.

If it takes twenty-one days to make a habit, how many days does it take to unmake a habit?

Several years ago Doris took up a new habit – regular exercise. She wondered why she hadn't done it several years earlier. She felt better, had more energy and was much more productive. Now Doris realizes that creating positive habits and eliminating negative habits is one of the most powerful methods for personal transformation and success. In fact, *successful people have habits that lead to success.*

People used to say that Henry Ford, the industrialist, was a very lucky man. But his friends said the funny thing was that the harder he worked, the luckier he got. For Henry it was not just hard work, it was a habit. How many times must he have gone into his office and spent long hours working on building his business? Henry did not just work hard off and on. He made a *habit* of working hard.

Ford perhaps exemplifies the fact that the more we put in, the more we tend to get out of life. And *where* we put our efforts is, more often than not, where we get our rewards. Is it any wonder then that some people's careers flourish while their relationships flounder?

An old saying about relationships is that *"the same thing it takes to get 'em, is the same thing it takes to keep 'em"*. Early on in relationships we usually put in a good deal of effort to make a good impression. But how often do we get lazy and fall out of earlier good habits in our relationships?

We get bored or start to take those relationships for granted. We stop bringing home what we used to bring home in the first place – be it flowers or just a positive outlook. Often we put in a better effort at the front end of something when it is new – maybe in a new relationship or a new role in our lives – but then we don't sustain that effort and fall out of our habits.

While working with a non-government development organization in India both of us learned many important lessons about life. In developing countries, the problems of health care, poverty and welfare can look insurmountable. It is very easy to perceive problems as being out of control and spiraling down fast.

The organization we worked with was working collaboratively with the local people to establish what was needed and how to get it. In the village planning sessions many difficult problems would arise. When trying to solve these problems, considerable effort was often directed towards establishing the underlying causes of the problems. In identifying these causes three important rules always applied:

- Lack of money is not the problem.
- Lack of time is not the problem.
- Other people are not the problem.

These simple, yet important, rules allowed energy to be focused creatively on those things that could be changed. It was not possible to blame the local bank (money), the short crop-growing season (time) or the government (other people) for the village's problems. This constructive approach reinforced to people that things were not outside the village's control. They had the power to do something.

These rules are also useful in thinking about making better decisions and building better habits. Money, time and other people are not the problem.

So how do we create successful, sustainable habits?

FORCE FIELD ANALYSIS

Forces have an impact on our ability to retain old habits or to establish new ones. By understanding these forces we can find ways to establish habits that will allow us to achieve our personal goals.

Force field analysis is a method for understanding forces that create and break habits. It works like this:

- Start by thinking of all the new habits you would like to develop and all the old habits you would like to break.
- Pick one new habit you would like to develop. Draw up a force field analysis diagram similar to the one on page 194. Write the habit at the top of the diagram.
- Now write down all the *driving forces* on the left-hand side of the status quo line. Driving forces are the forces that would make you take up the habit. Put an arrow next to each driving force. Make the length of the arrow equivalent to the intensity of the force. In this way, stronger driving forces will have longer arrows.
- Next, write down all the *restraining forces* on the right-hand side of the status quo line. Restraining forces are the forces which stop you from taking up the habit. Again, put an arrow under each restraining force and indicate the intensity by the length of the arrow. An example is shown below.
- To adopt the new habit you increase driving forces and decrease restraining forces, so select a number of major driving forces and create an action plan to increase these drivers. You can make the statement, "I could increase this driving force by …" For example, "I can *increase* the influence of … by …"
- Next, select a number of major restraining forces and create an action plan to decrease these drivers. You can make the statement, "I could decrease this restraining force by …" For example, "I can *decrease* the influence of … by …"

Habit: regular exercise

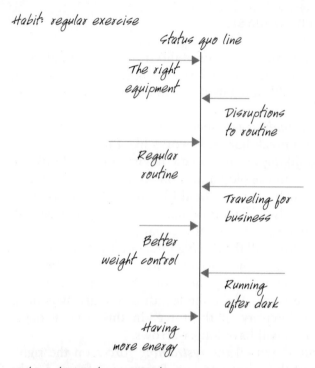

Status quo line

The right
equipment

Disruptions
to routine

Regular
routine

Traveling for
business

Better
weight control

Running
after dark

Having
more energy

Actions to create new habit
1   Purchase running shoes
2   Read up on benefits of exercise
3   Regular weight monitoring
4   Run at lunch time, not just in evening
5   Take exercise clothes when traveling for business

You now have an action plan for creating a new positive habit. Using this method you can work through the other new habits and create action plans for each.

Alternatively, you can use force field analysis to destroy old habits.

• Select one old habit you would like to destroy. Write the habit at the top of the blank force field analysis diagram.

• Now write down all the driving forces on the left-hand side of the status quo line. Driving forces are the forces that support the habit. Put an arrow under each driving force. Make the length of the arrow equivalent to the intensity of the force. Stronger driving forces will have longer arrows.

- Next, write down all the restraining forces on the right-hand side of the status quo line. Restraining forces resist the habit. Again, put an arrow under each restraining force and indicate the intensity by the length of the arrow.

- To stop an old habit you *decrease* driving forces and *increase* restraining forces, so select a number of major driving forces and create an action plan to decrease these drivers. You can make the statement, "I could decrease this driving force by ..." For example, "I can decrease the influence of ... by ..."

- Next, select a number of major restraining forces and create an action plan to increase these drivers. You can make the statement, "I could increase this restraining force by ..." For example, "I can increase the influence of ... by ..."

You now have an action plan to stop an old habit. Using this method you can work through other old habits and create action plans for each.

HABIT MIGRATION

Everybody at work agrees that Paul is a great guy to work with. He knows all the latest jokes and office gossip. He's always ready for a drink after work or to go out for lunch. He's active in the social club and clearly enjoys every aspect of his job.

Of course, Paul's great to have on your project team. He knows the organization back to front and has contacts everywhere. At work Paul is a model citizen.

At home, well, it's another matter. He's moody and unpredictable. Sometimes he gets angry over the smallest little thing. His wife, Clara, loves him deeply, but finds it difficult to cope at times. She's often glad when he leaves for work in the morning.

Paul's habits at work are quite different to his habits at home, to the detriment of his relationship with his wife.

In addition to destroying old habits and creating new ones, we can *migrate* our good habits from one sphere (or key content area) of our lives and apply them to another. We have called this *habit migration.*

We have picked work and home as an example, but you can use this method for any two areas of your life. You could even look at one area where you have really great habits and move these across to *all* other areas of your life.

Let's look at two types of habits: the way you treat people and the things you do. To start, consider the following question: "What would happen if I treated the people at work the way I treat the people at home...and the people at home the way I treat the people at work?" And, "What would happen if I did the things at work which I do at home...and did the things at home which I do at work?"

If you wish, draw up something like the page opposite to think about these two questions. Draw a line with an arrow where you would like to add a habit or activity from one sphere to another. For example:

What I do at work that I don't do at home	What I do at home that I don't do at work
Make a list of things to do at the start of the day →	Add to home habits
Add to work habits ←	Only drink strong coffee in the morning

Try this activity for habits in each of your key content areas. Where are your good habits and which ones could be useful in some other part of your life?

How I treat people at work that is different to the way I treat people at home	How I treat people at home that is different to the way I treat people at work

What I do at work that I don't do at home	What I do at home that I don't do at work

You can now use force field analysis to help you move this habit across. Alternatively, you can think about how to commit to this existing habit in a different sphere of your life.

Many people find this activity powerful because it creates consistency between the different dimensions of their lives.

As we have previously mentioned, better choices and habits are those choices and habits that are in alignment with our personal values. In fact, they are choices which are informed by our values. Furthermore, important decisions should reinforce and strengthen those values we hold as integral to who we are or who we wish to be. Our decisions and habits will then transform us and strengthen us as individuals.

Our decisions should also be directed to our life's purpose and to improving the quality of our relationships. Then we will be centered and purposeful in our lives. This approach to decision-making integrates meaning and action and this is, in many ways, the essence of success with soul.

Our values, life's purpose, decisions, plans, actions and personal reflection become key components of the dynamic system which is our mind, body and soul. Alignment and integration of these components provides depth to everything we do and meaning is created through the active structured dialogue of these components and through the establishment of relationships with other people and the world as a whole.

CHAPTER THIRTEEN

CREATIVE SOLUTIONS
TO "BALANCE" PROBLEMS

IN CHAPTER 7, we began to look beyond balance to solve problems of competing priorities in our lives. We said that systems thinking was a better approach for looking at these priorities, and that when we begin to understand that our lives are systems in dynamic tension we can start to find new, creative solutions. At this point, having looked at making better choices and building better habits, it is timely to revisit systems thinking and some of the methods arising from it.

> It's dangerous to leap a chasm in two bounds.
>
> *Chinese proverb*

Five methods arising from systems thinking are:
- integration
- elimination
- redefinition
- substitution
- acceptance.

Together these methods provide us with creative approaches for solving problems of competing priorities and dealing with tensions in our lives. They are all about examining our values and our life's purpose to determine creative solutions. These five methods for dealing with tensions are shown in the following matrix.

Methods matrix

Integration	Elimination
Redefinition	Substitution
Acceptance	

INTEGRATION

The process of integration brings together the two competing priorities, thereby reducing the tension in the system.

Often an integration strategy can significantly change the look of your current situation. Let's use integration to look again at the difficult issue of work and family.

Integration says the tension between work and family can be reduced by bringing the two closer together. Some specific integration strategies for work and family include working from home one or two days a week or bringing work home on the weekends rather than going into the office. Having lunch or coffee with a family member during the working week may be another way in which some degree of integration may be achieved.

These strategies can help ease the tension between work and family by ensuring we spend more time with the family without our work suffering. In fact, these strategies can help our work improve by providing us with a welcome break or change of environment.

The greatest degree of integration combines these two aspects of our lives into a new whole. The two are no longer in competition, but become part of each other. Two people working together in the same office is an example of this method of integration. The family that runs, say, a local store together is another example. The family shares the work and the common goal of supporting itself and its business. The children learn about working in the business while the parents get to watch their children grow and learn. This is very different to a situation where one or both parents work full-time outside the home.

Some integration strategies can take years to achieve. They can require significant planning and commitment. A long-term integration strategy was the method we chose to resolve a number of our relationship issues.

For some years, Stephen worked for an engineering consulting company and traveled about four months of the year. At the same time, Doris was working long hours for a major financial institution. We were also living in an old house that we were renovating at the time. It was a tough time and the relationship suffered. There were frequent arguments. One partner often blamed the other for the problems that existed. There was plenty of resentment and frustration regarding a range of issues and neither of us could see a way forward.

Divorce and relationship break-ups were frequent among employees in Stephen's industry and during his time with the company a number of marriages broke up under the strain of busy work schedules that kept families apart. In our case, it was probably our sheer stubbornness and pig-headedness not to let it happen to us that kept us going through that period.

After trying a range of solutions that failed, slowly, together, we began to see that the real solution lay in the long-term goal of working together in our own consulting business. As part of our annual planning session, we discussed this goal and how we could integrate the home, work and family key content areas of our lives. We also realized that some major changes would be required to achieve this goal.

Not only would Stephen have to change jobs, he would have to commit to a major career change. Doris would also have to change jobs and modify her career direction while committing to some additional study. We realized this process would take about five years to achieve, maybe longer.

Along the way it was vital to stay focused and committed to our long-term vision. During the transition period, Stephen was offered significant work opportunities which could easily have led in other career directions. Doris ended up changing jobs three times, rather than only once, over what ended up being a difficult period. A number of extremely stressful life events got in the way and threatened to block our vision. Partially as a result of these events, the move to self-employment took longer than we had hoped.

Now we work together in our own business and feel we have fairly successfully started to integrate home, work and family. The difficulty and hardship we experienced has made us even more appreciative of it all finally coming together.

This strategy has required significant compromise, sacrifice, persistence and hard work to turn a vision into a reality. However, it has provided both of us with a way to pursue career interests without sacrificing the family dimension of our lives.

Of course, we are not saying that this is the answer for everyone. A number of the people we know do not wish to work side by side with their partner or other members of their family all day. They find that work provides their relationship with some appreciated space. As always, it is up to each individual, partnership or family to determine what works for them.

Finally, let's look at one other application of integration strategies – resolving career and personal priorities.

From a very early age, Jon was fascinated by old things: antique furniture, old knick-knacks and some of the beautiful old silver his mother kept. His interest was first sparked by a gift his father once received as a visiting diplomat to Asia. The gift was a pair of ancient Chinese Ming Dynasty vases. Jon would sit staring at them; the intricate colors and designs, the beautiful curves. They seemed exotic and elusive sitting in the glass cabinet near the fireplace in their sitting room. He wondered where they had been and who had owned them all those years.

From this early interest, Jon started collecting old bits and pieces from second-hand stores and yard sales. The stuff would pile up in his room: coins and silverware, lamps, pieces of interesting dinnerware and small fossils. Jon could remember where each piece came from and would research interesting pieces to find out more about their background.

When he finished school, he went to college and eventually majored in archaeology. During this time, he developed an even greater passion for his interest. However, having finished his course he faced the difficult question, "What am I going to do for a living?" An arts major in archaeology was not going to open too many employers' doors.

To make matters worse, a number of friends and relatives suggested he consider antiques a hobby, one he could fund via a well-paying professional job. They suggested he go back to college and do a second course, perhaps in commerce or accounting. This did not appeal to Jon, but he knew he could make a good income from these professions. He was in a dilemma.

Around the time he was considering a second course, he visited one of his favorite antique shops where he talked to the owner, Albert, about his personal dilemma. Albert suggested that, rather than start another course, he should pursue his passion. One option he suggested was getting involved in buying antiques and selling them to antique shops. Albert explained how he bought the stock for his shop from a range of specialist buyers and importers, some of whom took buying trips to countries like India, China and Africa. Albert advised him: "Follow your heart, not your wallet."

This timely advice led Jon to begin his career in antiques and antiquities. As Albert suggested, he began in a small way by buying antiques for sale to antique shops. Over time, he started to develop a base of his own direct clients. Slowly this grew and grew. Now he has opened his own shop and is well on his way to becoming a recognized expert in his chosen field.

It didn't happen overnight. It took ten years of hard work. In the beginning he had to work part-time in factory jobs to support himself, while his friends in the professions enjoyed comfortable office jobs and high incomes. Today, however, many of them envy him working in an area he loves so much.

ELIMINATION

Elimination is another method derived from taking a systems thinking approach for managing competing priorities. While this method is not always easy, it is often very effective. Elimination means simply eliminating one of the "nodes", thereby eliminating the tension. For example, the tension between health and the pleasure of smoking can be resolved by the elimination of smoking.

Smoking — Health

Alfonse was a very family-oriented person whose family operated out of a very different set of values to his own – values he couldn't tolerate. At family gatherings he would find himself saying or doing things that went against his values, like boasting about a recent trip overseas or a promotion at work. This was not really his way, but it seemed to be the only type of conversation that his family was interested in. Eventually the alienation he felt from his family's values led to an enormous change in Alfonse's life.

Alfonse and his wife were young when they married. In those days it was expected that this was what you would do. They had children shortly after – three in all – and Alfonse always worked hard and was a good provider. They lived in a neighborhood where everyone was reasonably friendly and they had many friends close by. They entertained at home as well as going out to visit.

On the surface it all seemed idyllic. However, something had never seemed quite right from Alfonse's perspective. He had traveled widely in his job, both interstate and overseas. During his life he had mixed with people he found fascinating and like-minded. He found the people in his family and neighborhood narrow-minded and bigoted by comparison. Worse than this, he felt that his wife also shared these characteristics.

Some years ago he started to discuss these issues with his wife. He explained that he felt out of place and wanted to be with people he felt more comfortable with. She had known for some time that he was unhappy, but she was very happy where she was, although her relationship with Alfonse had grown cold. They agreed to stay together until the children had grown up and left home.

At the age of forty-five, Alfonse left his wife and they filed for divorce. He left the country and settled down in Australia, where he felt at home and could mix with people who shared his values. It had been a tough decision and his friends and family back home blamed him for breaking up the family. But for Alfonse, eliminating an environment out of touch with his values had been the right decision.

REDEFINITION

The way in which we define something often influences the way in which we think about it. For example, when we define a brisk walk as exercise, we influence how we think about walking briskly by associating it with exercise. If we have a positive attitude to exercise, it follows that we will probably have a positive attitude to a brisk walk. If, however, we think about exercise as boring and unappealing, then we are likely to feel the same about a brisk walk.

If we *redefine* something, we can also change the way we think about it. For example, if we don't exercise regularly but we do like to spend time thinking about interesting issues, we can redefine our brisk walk as, say, "an opportunity to get out of the house and think". In this way we are likely to change our attitude towards walking and perhaps exercise.

People use this method with children. A teaspoon of medicine may be redefined as an airplane, and the child's mouth as the airplane hangar. "Here comes the airplane. Open up the hangar!" often works better for getting medicine in the mouth than saying, "Open your mouth and take your medicine!" The method works because the child thinks about what is happening in a new and more positive way.

Another example is redefining housework as exercise. In this way, housework could be seen as a substitute for a trip to the gym.

Housework ● —— Gym

Redefinition is also an important method for managing social and economic issues. One important example today is the tension between a company's need for efficient production and people's need for meaningful work.

Need for meaningful work • ——— ∿∿∿∿∿∿ ——— • Need for efficient production

It is a relatively well-known fact that most large companies today are "downsizing", shedding staff in efforts to achieve more cost-effective production, thereby increasing their competitiveness. In addition, new technology has provided machines and equipment that have replaced large numbers of employees. The number of unemployed and under-employed people is rising steadily and is unlikely to reduce again.

However, without meaningful work, people become disillusioned and depressed. As the founder of psychotherapy, Sigmund Freud, once said, the two things that humans need are love and work. The human cost of unemployment is enormous, sometimes spilling over into crime and violence.

One strategy being actively explored for managing this tension is the "redefinition of work". If work in the private and public sectors is going to continue to decrease, then perhaps one solution is to extend our definition of work to include voluntary work conducted for the community sector.

A number of economic forecasters, such as Jeremy Rifkin in his book *The End of Work*, see the writing on the wall. They are strongly recommending incentives for work in the community sector.

People and organizations already receive tax deductions for money donated to the community sector, and there are calls for a similar incentive system for hours of work donated. The community sector is crying out for workers, in contrast to the public and private sectors...and this certainly fulfills the criterion of providing *meaningful* work. Some economic forecasters suggest that if we redefine time volunteered in the community sector as work, we may begin successfully to address this increasing tension.

SUBSTITUTION

A fourth strategy for managing tensions is substitution. Substitution is based on the principle that some competing priorities can be traded off against each other. Let's look at how substitution works with a common issue – the tension between time and money.

Time • ——— {{{{{{{{{- ——— • Money

Have you noticed the way time and money are often in tension in your life? When *we trade our time for money* by working we have less time for other activities. In this situation, we can become *money rich and time poor.*

Conversely, when we spend less time working, we usually have less money. However, we do have more time for non-work activities. In this situation, we may become *money poor and time rich*.

All of this arises because, on a basic level, *we trade our time for money*, so time and money are interchangeable resources. The fact is, we often have the flexibility *to use time to create money or money to create time*.

To start with, here are some strategies that free up more time – time to spend on those things you would like to do.

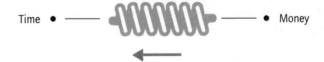

Consider the following question: "What do I spend time on that I don't like doing or that provides me with little meaning?" Write some of these down if you like. It may include doing housework, gardening, lawn-mowing or paying bills.

Now, think about how you can use money to reduce or even to remove this activity from your life. It may be paying someone to assist you at work, or someone to assist you at home with tasks like cleaning, paying bills or doing housework. All these strategies use money to buy you more time to do the things you want to do.

Conversely, let's look at a situation where you feel you don't have enough money, but you have (or could make) some extra time, time which could be used to make additional money.

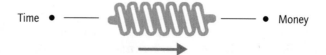

Time ●　——　〰〰〰〰〰〰〰　——　● Money

Strategies to substitute time for money include working more overtime, taking a job or a second job if you already have one, or putting in more hours at work.

Sometimes time is not freely available either. You may have a great many time commitments outside of the time committed to earning money. More creative solutions are then required. One example would be to have someone you know take over some of the non-paying tasks you need to do, to free up your time to do paying work.

You may say that this is all pretty obvious. In many ways it is. However, it does raise an important question: *What is your time really worth?*

People who are paid by the hour know the monetary value of their work time. If you work for a fixed salary you can work out the monetary value of your work time by the hour.

But what is your non-work time worth? What is time on your hobbies worth? What is time with your partner or family worth? It must be worth something, so put a dollar value on it.

Now, what has the highest value? Does your time with your family, on your hobbies or with your partner have a higher value than what you are paid to do at work? If the answer is yes, then maybe it's time to use some of your money to buy more time for these important things.

Some parents must pay for childcare because for financial reasons they must work. However, many other parents pay someone to look after their children part-time so they can continue to work in jobs that they enjoy. For many of these parents, what they earn and what they pay someone else for childcare may not be all that different. Nonetheless, they buy themselves some time to continue doing the work they want to do.

ACCEPTANCE

Acceptance is sometimes the most difficult way to deal with tensions in our lives. Acceptance means that we don't change what we do. Instead, we change our attitude to it.

Importantly, the option to accept things the way they are is always available to us. For example, few people are ever really happy with how much money they have. No matter what they earn, it never seems to be enough. This is partially due to people's ability to spend up to and beyond what they earn. We live in a consumer society which encourages us to do so. However, an acceptance strategy for our sanity is to accept what we currently earn and learn to live within our means.

Acceptance is not the "head in the sand" approach, where we ignore the consequences of a decision to live with things the way they are. It is not a lazy approach, where we put off solving important issues because we don't want to deal with them. When we use acceptance as a strategy, we do so consciously, with an awareness of the repercussions of our decision.

This strategy works particularly well when you have a long-term goal. In the story of Beverley in chapter 3, Beverley had tension between her current job and her relationship with her partner. Once she had developed a long-term strategy it was possible for her to accept her current situation and concentrate on resolving the outstanding issues with her partner.

Finally, we sometimes learn acceptance when we are placed in a situation beyond our control.

Many years ago when we were traveling in India, we arrived in the city of Agra, home of the famous Taj Mahal. We were exhausted after two days' travel by train, bus and cab. The mid-summer heat was oppressive, made even more unbearable by a hot, dry wind coming off the desert. It was midday, the hottest part of the day. Sweat trickled down the back of our burnt and dusty necks.

A short auto-rickshaw ride was the final leg of a long journey that brought us to our motel near the South Gate of the Taj Mahal. The motel was run by an elderly Indian couple who kept the tiny, spartan motel neat and clean.

As we checked in, all we could think of was a cool shower and a long rest under a ceiling fan. Quite suddenly, the electrical power went off in that part of city – an unfortunately common occurrence in Agra, as we later found out. The Indians had a quaint phrase for it, too – load shedding – as if to suggest the system had *too much electricity*! To make matters worse, we learned that without power the pump for the shower didn't work and, of course, the ceiling fans were out of action. Desperate happenings indeed.

Dirty, hot and tired, we dumped our bags in our room, wandered out of the sweltering motel lobby and sat in the courtyard with the old man who ran the motel. He was a tall, thin fellow, dressed in little more than a cloth around his middle. He looked like a wise old man with a composed, mystical air about him. He could see that we were tired and having trouble coming to terms with the recent turn of events. He looked at us and then spoke clearly and very slowly: "It is hot... and there is no power... and there is no water..." It was a simple statement of fact. It was also a message that acceptance was required, the only option available in fact. We nodded slowly and somehow felt freed from the feeling that something was wrong and that something should happen. We felt calmer and more at peace. Acceptance can be a great relief and an effective strategy.

APPLYING THE FIVE STRATEGIES

We have looked at five strategies arising out of systems thinking for dealing with tensions and contradictions in our lives – integration, elimination, redefinition, substitution and acceptance. What follows is a simple activity that shows how these strategies can be used.

First, think of one or two competing priorities which create tension in your life. If you identified several competing priorities when you developed your statements of purpose in chapter 10, you may wish to use those. Once you have selected the priorities you wish to consider, draw them on a tension diagram with one of the two priorities at each end.

Next, underneath the tension diagram, draw up a matrix like the one below. Now try to identify the strategies available to manage these competing priorities better. Spend 10–20 minutes brainstorming as many as you can. Make sure you spend time thinking about strategies based on each of the five methods. Write them in the boxes in the matrix you have drawn. It is important to note that not every one of the five methods works in every situation. There may be only two or three methods that are useful in any given situation.

Next, thinking about the specific strategies you have identified, consider the following questions:

- What are the strengths and weaknesses of each strategy?
- What is the long-term impact of each strategy? Do the strategies help me achieve my personal strategic plan?
- Do any strategies contradict my personal values or my life's purpose?
- Which strategies am I willing to commit to?
- Can a number of strategies be used together to achieve a better overall solution?

Competing priorities

Methods matrix

Integration	Elimination
Redefinition	Substitution
Acceptance	

This chapter has presented a range of methods for dealing with contradictions and tensions in our lives. As we implement some of these methods or any of the others presented in this book, we can increase the effectiveness of our planning and actions by the use of evaluation. The next chapter discusses methods for feedback, monitoring and reflection that we can apply to the planning and actions in our lives.

CHAPTER FOURTEEN

FEEDBACK, MONITORING AND REFLECTION

MOST ORGANIZATIONS have a range of feedback, monitoring and reflection processes in place to assess their performance. For example, staff may receive a regular performance appraisal from their manager. During this appraisal, each person receives *feedback* on their performance over the past few months or year. This process provides them with information on how they can improve in the future and tells them how other people are reacting to them.

Similarly, organizations *monitor* variables such as sales and revenue. They use important indicators to keep track of how they are going.

Many organizations also have retreats where management and staff leave their everyday workplace to *reflect* and think about "the big picture".

> Mental reflection is so much more interesting than TV it's a shame more people don't switch over to it.
> They probably think what they hear is unimportant but it never is.
>
> *Robert M. Pirsig*

Strangely, many of us experience these dynamics in our work environment, yet we don't even think of incorporating them into our personal lives. All successful endeavors, including both personal and corporate, require feedback, monitoring and reflection. These dynamics help us stay on track and heading in the direction we wish to go.

Imagine driving a car out of town, maybe just to get away for the day or to visit a friend you haven't seen in some time.

You check the road map and then start the car. It's a sunny afternoon and soon the traffic clears, leaving you alone on the open road.

Suspend reality for a moment and imagine that while you are driving you decide to close your eyes, just for a second. What would happen? Most likely nothing serious or danger-ous. The road is straight and the car has plenty of momentum in a straight line. Now what if you close your eyes for one second and take your hands off the wheel at the same time? The car may move slightly to the left or right depending on the road surface, but the odds are you will still be okay.

However, what if you took your hands off the wheel and closed your eyes for two seconds or three seconds? Things are now starting to get pretty dangerous. In fact, if you continued to increase the time without feedback from the car it would eventually run off the road or miss a turn.

It's the same with life – to achieve personal success we need a road map *and* feedback, monitoring and personal reflection to make sure we reach our desired destinations. Without these three activities we will eventually run into trouble. If we are lucky we may just miss a turnoff and find ourselves somewhere we had not planned to go. If we are not so lucky we may end up off the road entirely.

So let's look at feedback, monitoring and personal reflection in more detail and understand how they can help us achieve personal success. We will also look at some specific methods and techniques that we can all use at the personal level, techniques that build on the other methods we have already discussed, for example the life circle and personal journey timeline.

FEEDBACK

Feedback tells us how a system is functioning. For example, when we drive a car or ride a bicycle, we get feedback through our eyes, arms and body. This feedback provides us with information about the performance of the system that we are part of, and helps us to make necessary adjustments.

Sometimes feedback comes to us without our seeking it. It may be a natural part of the system. When we get a flat tyre we usually feel a difference in handling that alerts us to the problem. This is feedback. However, at other times we need actively to seek feedback. We need to assess the impact of our actions on the system. For example, sometimes when we have prepared a meal for someone, we ask them for their feedback.

As we have previously discussed, our life is part of a system, and collecting feedback can tell us a great deal about our interactions within the system in which we live. This system includes the people around us and our environment. For example, we may learn about the adjustments we need to make to our actions and habits to achieve our plans. We can also learn which of our actions support our long-term goals and which actions do not.

The two main ways to collect feedback are:
- observation
- request.

Because so much feedback is available and comes to us without requesting it, we simply need to be observant and open to it. Doris remembers baking a nutritious fruit and nut cake several years ago. Friends came around for coffee and she offered them each a piece. Watching the expressions on their faces and the effort that seemed to go into eating it, she soon gathered that it was probably a little too chewy! She didn't have to ask – their faces said it all.

Sometimes, though, we need actively to seek feedback, and one of the best ways is simply to ask for it. Other people are an excellent source of feedback and often they see things that are not obvious to us.

Many companies use the principle of feedback as part of their staff performance appraisal process. They ask each person's peers, manager and staff to provide feedback on the performance of that person. This may include specific feedback on work performance, communication skills and displayed leadership. These methods are sometimes called "360-degree feedback".

The 360-degree feedback model reminds us that when we seek feedback it is important to think about who we should seek feedback from and what their biases might be. Your partner's view of your actions might be very different to that of your boss or another work colleague.

The kinds of questions we could ask people to get feedback might include:

• What were your impressions of my presentation?
• Did you think my performance was good or bad?
• Did you like or dislike what I did?
• What do you think I could have done differently?
• How could I do it better next time?

Asking for feedback has other positive effects apart from providing us with information about ourselves. One of the most important impacts of asking for feedback is that it creates trust. When we ask for feedback we demonstrate our openness to another person's judgment. In this way, seeking feedback can strengthen our relationships with others. Moreover, creating the impression that we are open to feedback increases the likelihood that people around us will volunteer feedback, rather than us always having to ask for it.

Monitoring

Monitoring tells us where we are and what progress we have made. For example, when we read the signposts and milestones beside the road, we determine where we are on our journey and how far we have traveled. Monitoring is important because it tells us about how we are progressing compared to our plans, in particular our personal strategic plans. Monitoring considers the questions, "How am I going?" and "What progress have I made?"

Monitoring is different to feedback. Feedback is about how we interact in the system. Monitoring is specifically about how we are progressing relative to our own goals and purpose.

Monitoring involves some form of measurement, either quantitative or qualitative.

Quantitative measurements use numbers. For example, when you check your bank balance, that's a quantitative measurement. By comparison, qualitative measurements use words or pictures. "Are you going well in your job?" or "How is your life going at the moment?" are both questions that elicit qualitative answers.

While we frequently monitor quantitative variables in our lives like bank balances and salaries, many of the most important things in life are not measurable by quantitative measures. Emotions, values and motivations are all difficult to quantify. Words and pictures provide us with better ways to express and hence measure these variables.

Let's now look at some specific methods for monitoring your progress.

WHOLE SYSTEM MAP

One of the problems with the ways many of us monitor our progress in life is that we are very tactical about it. We look at the size of our salary or our progress on paying off our house. We look at how well our diet is going or whatever. We tend to look at each of these factors in isolation, forgetting that we are operating in a whole system.

The classic example, as we have discussed throughout this book, is measuring career progress in isolation from everything else in our lives. Sometimes, in ignoring the whole system, we fail to see that as career performance gets better and better, all the other areas of our lives are getting worse and worse. The "antidote" to non-systems thinking is to build on the tools we have learned so far in this book, tools which ensure a systemic approach to life.

The *whole system map* is a tool which has been developed for monitoring our progress. This tool uses your life circle as a basis and overlays a "map" showing your progress. This allows you to evaluate how you are going against each of your key content areas and your statements of purpose. This is how it works.

First, take your life circle and think about where in each of those key content areas you are at this point in your life. To help yourself focus, read over your statements of purpose for each area.

Now place a point in each key content area to represent your current performance. Assume the center of the circle is low or not so good, and the outer edge of the circle is high or very positive. Don't labor over each one too much. Your first impressions are probably the best to go with.

As an example, you might have one key content area called "Exercise". Think about how you would assess yourself on this dimension, say over the past few months. Have you exercised as frequently as you might wish to? Did you set goals for exercising and how have you performed relative to these? How happy are you with your behavior or achievements in this dimension of your life? You might like to mark yourself on a scale of 1–10.

When you have worked through all of your key content areas, and plotted a point for each of them on your life circle, join the points to create a shape. The circle below is an example of how your life circle might look once you have drawn your shape.

This map which you have overlaid over your life circle is your current *whole system map* – a way to monitor your "whole life system". This map is extremely data rich. Not only does it tell you your performance in each of your key content areas, it provides you with a picture of the whole system, including information on how the whole system is working.

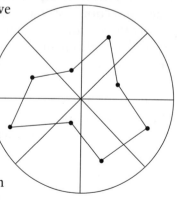

Are you performing extremely well in one area so that that area is "pulling" the others in, causing a skew to one side? Are there one or two areas you feel you really want to put extra effort into?

If you wish you can give your map a title. For example, "My map is like a ..."

When you look at the shape of your whole system map, consider the following questions:

- Does anything surprise you about the shape?
- Are there tensions between segments? Where?
- How do you feel about the shape?
- What would you like to change?
- How could you make the total shape bigger?

This is the big picture. You can extend your monitoring to more detailed analysis of each key content area. What criteria do you use to monitor your performance in each of these areas? What are the more quantitative measures of your progress in each area?

PERSONAL REFLECTION

Personal reflection considers broader and deeper issues than feedback and monitoring. Personal reflection allows us to explore important questions such as, "What have I learned about myself from my personal journey?" and "Is this still the right direction for me?" Personal reflection probes more deeply than feedback and monitoring. It invites us to question ourselves and our plans, to look at our values, motivations and emotions.

The personal journey timeline activity in chapter 8 is a method for personal reflection. The timeline activity is a structured method for reflecting on our experiences, feelings and values. We can use this activity at any time in our lives. It can be used to paint a picture of:

- your whole life from birth to the present
- the last five years

- the past twelve months
- the past month
- the past week
- the day you have just had.

We use the personal journey timeline on our annual planning retreat. Before going on to do our whole system map for the year, we paint a picture of the whole past year. This ensures we have all the events, feelings, thoughts and decisions of the year clear in our minds before we start to reassess our key content areas and statements of purpose, and before going on to plan the next twelve months.

The personal journey timeline activity is a structured method of personal reflection. Without structure, personal reflection can often lead us to poor conclusions and decisions.

> John, who is forty-five, is a manager with a Fortune 500 company. He went to see a therapist recently regarding problems he was having. The therapist asked John to explain his difficulties.
>
> John considered the question for a while and then responded. "Well, I'm going nowhere. My career is in a mess. I think I'll just resign. Yes, that's what I'll do and then worry about what I am going to do later. I need some space to sort things out. I mean, I feel useless in my job. I get angry and I feel really down a lot of the time. Well, I did get a promotion recently so they must have thought I was doing something right and I got a pay rise too. But what's the point, there's no meaning in this stuff for me."
>
> The therapist was not quite sure what to make of all of this. It all seemed very confusing. And it was – for John, too.
>
> The therapist then took John through a structured method for personal reflection. Using this method, John was able clearly to understand his situation and then to formulate some constructive responses to it.

The four-step reflection method

The four-step reflection method is a powerful tool for structured personal reflection. This thinking process leads us from surface observations of a situation, through recognizing our emotions and feelings, to in-depth understanding, and finally to a decision or response.

The four steps in this personal reflection method are the objective, reflective, interpretive and decisional. We learned this method many years ago from the Institute of Cultural Affairs who later described it in their book *Winning Through Participation*.

The *objective* step draws out the facts about the event or experience. We recall information about it and try to re-create it accurately in our minds. How we feel about the event or experience is the subject of the second or *reflective* step. Emotional responses and thought associations about the time or event are brought to the surface. In the third step, the *interpretive*, we consider the meaning and value of the event and the significance it has for us. The fourth step, the *decisional*, is where we formulate a response to the situation, determining what decision is necessary or what action is required.

The power of this method is that it ensures all the important aspects of personal reflection are covered *and* that these steps are covered in the most effective way. For example, we do not jump to conclusions or decisions without considering all the facts. Similarly, we do not focus solely on our emotional reaction to a situation.

Personal reflection method

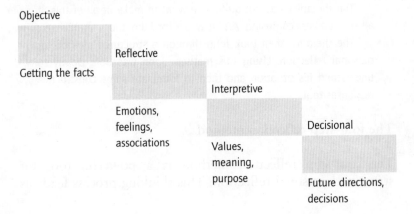

Objective

Reflective

Getting the facts

Interpretive

Emotions,
feelings,
associations

Decisional

Values,
meaning,
purpose

Future directions,
decisions

It is fascinating that this little-used method is actually a natural process. To illustrate how natural this process is, imagine you have just arrived home from work and it's time for dinner. These are the facts: "It's dinner time. I had a long day with a meeting all afternoon." Then comes the emotional response: "I'm really tired tonight and I'm feeling a bit down after the meeting."

Then you interpret the situation: "I'm too tired to cook something tonight. I could just get something quick out of the freezer – but I'm sure I'd get depressed sitting eating it in front of the TV. I could go get something from the pizza place and bring it back. I feel like some company so maybe I could ring Pete and go grab something to eat out with him."

Finally, you decide on a course of action: "I am going to call Pete and ask him if he wants to go out for a quick bite. If he isn't in I'll call Anne or Bob. And I think I'll ask someone over for dinner tomorrow night too while I think of it."

Now we will work through the four stages in some more detail.

The first stage is the objective stage. This stage draws out the facts from a particular experience or event. Information and details help re-create the experience or event in your mind. At the objective level, opinions and judgments are put on hold while "the facts" are gathered. In this way, we develop an *objective* picture of the situation and ensure all relevant information is in front of us.

Without this first step we may focus on how we feel about the situation without thinking through all the facts first, like John who first said, "I hate my job." However, when John thought at the objective level first, he put things into perspective. He identified the different aspects of his job and the key relationships he had with his boss and staff. He was then in a better position to understand his reactions to the current situation at the reflective level.

At the second stage, the reflective stage, emotional responses are acknowledged. How we feel, what we like and dislike are considered. Emotions and thought associations are brought into the open and *reflected* on.

When John says, "I feel useless. I get angry and I feel really down a lot of the time," he is responding at the reflective level. However, when the therapist asked John to consider his emotions in light of the objective facts, John began to see things differently. He identified many good things about his current job, despite his initial reactions, and he could also more clearly identify those parts of his current job he didn't like.

As discussed earlier, emotions are an important, but often unrecognized, aspect of effective decision-making. The reflective stage supports effective decision-making because it explores emotions.

The third stage is the interpretive stage. Here you *interpret* the meaning and value of the situation and its significance. This puts events and emotions into perspective and assesses their impact. In this way, we develop an understanding of our emotional reactions.

When John says, "My life is a mess. There's no meaning in this stuff for me," his thoughts are coming from the interpretive level. When the therapist helped John to interpret the facts and his emotional responses, John saw things differently. He could see his reaction to the problems with his new boss and the relationships to his old work colleagues. John was therefore better placed to make some rational decisions.

The fourth and final stage, the decisional stage, is where you conceive a response by *deciding* what action may be required. This final stage acts as the catalyst for moving forward rather than settling for opinions with no action.

John was operating at the decisional stage when he decided to resign to create some "space to sort things out".

When John worked logically through this structured method of personal reflection he made a set of decisions which were the best possible decisions at the time. Rather than resign, John decided to talk to his boss about some of the problems he was having. He also decided to delegate some of the work he was finding so frustrating and unsatisfying. Having been taught the structured personal reflection method, John could use it in the future to solve issues on his own.

This method – the four-step personal reflection method – provides a structure that guides you through four stages of critical thinking. The method is both simple and sophisticated. It is simple because, as shown, it is based on a natural process. It is sophisticated because it ensures that all relevant information and emotional responses are explored. It peels back the layers of our thinking, with each stage exploring a little deeper, until we arrive at the heart of any issue or situation. In this way, we avoid superficial conclusions. Our thoughts are clarified and our perspective broadens, allowing greater confidence in decision-making.

You may wonder why we need to be taught this process if it is so natural. Unfortunately, we are often taught or encouraged to short-cut this process – to jump straight to the interpretive or decisional stages.

One application of this method is to reflect on your life as it is now. The questions below take you through the four stages in the process. They allow you to look at the facts, think about how you feel about your life now, reflect on what it means, and finally to look at what decisions you might take. Just grab a piece of paper and write down each heading, followed by your answers. Alternatively, divide a sheet of paper into four quadrants, one for each stage of your personal reflection.

Objective
- What visual images come to mind about your life at the moment?
- What events come to mind?
- What words or phrases come to mind?
- Who are the people that come to mind?
- What do you see yourself doing?

Reflective
- What is the high point for you at the moment?
- What is the low point?
- What do you enjoy the most?
- What do you enjoy the least?
- Describe your mood generally.

Interpretive
- What have you learned about yourself recently?
- What do you think this period of time has taught you about other people?
- Why did you enjoy some aspects and not others?
- Why did you have those particular emotional responses?

Decisional
- What would you like to do differently?
- What would you like to do more of/less of?
- What could you do tomorrow to demonstrate that you had internalized your recent personal insights?
- What could you do to make your life better based on what you have learned from this reflection?

This method can be used in many situations. You can use it when having a conversation with a partner about a "touchy" issue where strong emotions are involved. Sticking to this structured method can help you work through the issues productively. Also, the four-step personal reflection method can be used to check if someone else sees a situation the same way you do.

Finally, personal reflection is best when *inspired* in some way. Inspiration for personal reflection can come from many sources. Sometimes experiences that are very *different* to our everyday experiences provide us with food for thought about our everyday lives – seeing the ways people live provides us with a different view of our own lives.

For many people, travel provides these sources of inspiration for personal reflection. When we visit or live in other cultures we experience a range of differences from our "at home" experiences. The food, customs, social conventions, government and religions may all be markedly different. Basic assumptions that we hold to be true are either not present or are turned upside-down.

Through our relationships with other people we are provided with the unique opportunity to learn about ourselves through observation and close personal questioning.

So travel widely, meet new people, do new things...that which is different is a mirror for personal reflection.

> Unanticipated invitations to travel are dancing lessons from God.
>
> *Kurt Vonnegut*

Feedback, monitoring and personal reflection together provide us with information about the key relationships we have with ourselves, other people and our environment. They help us to determine whether we are improving the quality of these relationships. In the next chapter we will look at a four-stage process to initiate creative change in your life. This process will be your catalyst for creating personal change.

> Unanticipated invitations to travel are dancing lessons from God.
>
> — Kurt von...

CHAPTER FIFTEEN

INITIATING
CREATIVE CHANGE

TRYING TO SQUEEZE creative personal reflection and planning around everyday activities generally fails. We discovered this for ourselves when we attempted to get our lives in order over ten years ago. Rather unimaginatively as it turned out, we decided to have a weekly family meeting, on Sunday nights, to discuss short-term and long-term issues. The aim of these regular meetings was to get organized for the busy week ahead and to plan for the future.

> Change is not made without inconvenience, even from worse to better.
>
> *Samuel Johnson*

The first few weeks went well. We dealt with a backlog of pressing short-term issues. Bills got paid, domestic duties were organized and assigned, and the house began to run smoothly. Our strategy appeared to be working quite well. Then we turned our attention to the long-term issues; career planning, setting a vision for the family, long-term financial concerns and so on. It was a disaster. The process didn't work at all. We had no real structure for resolving any of these types of issues. In addition, the time we had allowed to address them was insufficient and unsuitable. We were either relaxed after the weekend and didn't want to talk about "heavy" issues, or busy preparing for the coming week. After several unsatisfying months, we gave it away.

With the failure of our initial efforts, it took nearly two years to find the commitment and inspiration to try again, and then it was only because financial, domestic and relationship problems had pushed our marriage to breaking point. It was the last real chance.

We realized this time that we needed a more effective and creative method for resolving long-term issues. We needed to be sufficiently relaxed to reflect and plan without short-term urgent issues crowding out long-term issues. In addition, we needed to re-think what our long-term planning was really about. Was it for resolving problems, for family and financial management, or was it simply to keep the relationship together? In the end, we decided that these could be *outcomes* of the process, but that they should not be the primary focus. What we really needed was a process for *on-going creative personal change.*

This creative change would allow both of us to grow and, hopefully, for the relationship to grow with us. However, we realized that there was a risk in this strategy. We might grow apart in the process or find that we could not grow in a similar direction. It was a risk we had to take. As a good friend of ours says, "Sometimes you have to be willing to put your relationship on the line, in order to keep it."

As we now know, there are three important prerequisites before creative personal change is possible. These are described succinctly by John Hayes in his book *The Complete Problem Solver.* They are:
- sufficient interest to invest the time and energy to change
- sufficient personal confidence to believe that you are not simply wasting your time
- freedom from other responsibilities so that the necessary time is available to you.

Our original weekly meetings had clearly not satisfied all these prerequisites. To start with, we had not given ourselves enough freedom from other responsibilities to initiate creative change. As a result, we had lost confidence in our process, and finally we became unwilling to invest the time and energy.

INITIATING CREATIVE CHANGE

In our own case, through trial and error and a bit of commonsense, we eventually developed our own four-stage process for creative change. We later saw this process described by Lawrence Brammer in his book *How to Cope with Life Transitions: The Challenge of Personal Change.* The four steps to initiating creative personal change are:
- disruption
- incubation
- transformation
- action.

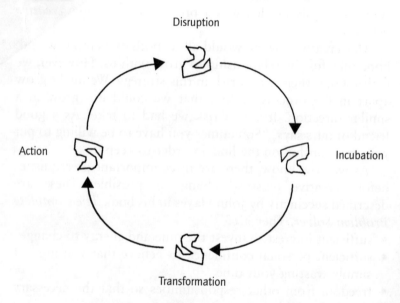

Let's look at these four stages in detail.

Disruption

The first stage, disruption, can occur in two different ways. First, we can disrupt our lives ourselves, by taking time out from what we normally do, by getting away from our everyday environment and its day-to-day issues. Alternatively, there are times when something intrudes or *disrupts* our lives from the outside. Either way, with our routine disrupted, ideas can come more freely and new possibilities emerge. We can also reflect more creatively on our lives when we have some distance from our normal activities.

Organizations are well aware of this. They often use corporate retreats as a disruption from the normal office routine. Away from the phone, the customers and the urgent everyday issues, reflection and long-term planning are easier. Energy can be focused and creativity harnessed.

Disruption also occurs when we go on vacation. While on holiday we often feel more creative. We may pursue more right-brain activities like taking photographs, trying new experiences (such as scuba diving, skiing and so on) or reading interesting books. In addition, we may come back from a holiday with many new ideas for our work. Commonly, these ideas are more creative than the ones we come up with during the normal course of work.

However, this disruption process is not enough on its own, and it has led to one of the myths about personal change – such as the idea that going away on the big trip to Europe or around the world will help you work out what you are going to do with your life. While it may appear to be a good idea, and it certainly is a pleasant disruption, it does not necessarily work. Disruption is only the first stage in the process. Unless there is some form of structured personal reflection in your travel, nothing is likely to happen. Your unresolved issues will still be there when you get home.

Annual holidays can be a good time to do some structured personal reflection. Plan to spend the first couple of days just clearing the head; then you are in the right state of mind to spend a little time reflecting and planning. "What a great way to spoil a good holiday," we hear you say. However, we believe this is partly what holidays are about: once a year spending time relaxing, reflecting and planning, using a couple of hours a day, say in the afternoons, to do some structured personal reflection and strategic planning, using processes such as the ones we have detailed in this book.

We use this process to do our planning every year. We get away somewhere if we can, to the beach or up to the hills, or we just take time out at home. We pull out our various planning tools – our life circles, our statements of purpose and our personal strategic plans. We then spend just a few days reflecting and creating our family's journey timeline for the past twelve months. We review our key content areas and statements of purpose. Finally, we revisit our twenty-year and five-year plans and develop our plan for the next twelve months.

A professional leave of absence or sabbatical is also an excellent method to disrupt your normal routine. Author and management guru Tom Peters says that if you have been working for five years without at least a six-month break you are probably stale. We can't always afford to take a six-month break, but his words are worth keeping in mind.

Finally, we believe that if you really want to embark on a process of personal change, don't only flick through this book – take yourself away, even if only for a couple of days, and really begin to make some personal change.

If you really can't get away, here is another creative idea for some disruption. What about taking a tape-recorder with you when you go for a run or a brisk walk? Rather than listening to other people's creativity – music, talkback radio and the like – press the record button and just talk. Record your thoughts about the kind of issues discussed in this book. You will have a great time if nothing else, and will be amazed at the insights that occur to you. All that oxygen pulsing around the brain can really make a difference.

Incubation

The second stage in initiating creative personal change is what psychologists call "the *incubation* period". Incubation is a quiet time for meditation and relaxation, or for recreational activities like walking and swimming. This is a time when it is better to do less, rather than more, and if someone asks you what is happening or what you are doing, the answer may simply be "nothing". However, this is not quite true.

Something *is* happening, but it is beneath our everyday consciousness. Our minds are going over the ideas and plans that we developed during the first stage of the change process. Ideas will quietly simmer – or boil, depending on the nature of the change.

During the incubation stage, it is best not to try to "push" or force ideas. The work done during the disruption stage has provided "grist for the mill". Now your mind will "mill" this new information, and new insights will start to formulate, new connections will start to be made. The best thing to do during this time is whatever you usually do for relaxation. It is best to keep things low key while your mind works through all of these new thoughts and ideas.

This can be a frustrating time – especially if we are keen to control a situation. Unfortunately during this stage there is very little we can control. Part of what occurs at the incubation stage is not open to us. It is somewhat mysterious. We must simply trust the process.

Transformation

Disruption and incubation ready us for the third stage in this creative change process: *transformation*. Now things become exciting. It is like the moment of taking a cake out of the oven. Something has been working on the ingredients and now it is time to see what has been created.

The transformation stage can be an insightful or "ah-hah" experience, when new ideas tumble over one another, and the world is seen differently. Often during this stage we see new opportunities, or our personal or business problems suddenly seem solvable.

In fact, this book resulted from a transformational experience. Doris woke up one night, about 3 a.m., sat bolt upright and suddenly knew we were going to put our ideas into some kind of product. It was a totally new, radically different idea for us. Up to that point we had always thought of ourselves as consultants. We had never produced a product before. Suddenly, after what had been a period of restlessness and incubation, a transformation occurred.

Interestingly, Doris's idea was not a dream. She didn't dream that we were going to do it. It was like her mind decided to wake her up and deliver a message. Her mind was the "marketing department" – it came up with an idea. It was then up to the rest of the "organization" to refine and develop the idea.

So how do we "get this to happen"? How can we experience this *transformation*? Well, it would be like taking a trip to see the wildlife on the plains of Africa. Initially, you would prepare yourself and read up on the places to go and where to stay. Once you were there, you would put yourself in more or less the right place and let it happen. Using this approach means that sometimes you find the wildlife, and other times the wildlife finds you. *In the same way, disruption and incubation prepare us to find ideas. Sometimes though, the ideas find us.*

This method works because it breaks up our regular patterns of behavior and puts us in the right frame of mind for thinking creatively about our lives. Some structured personal reflection allows us to make the most of the initial disruption stage, filling our minds with plenty of new ideas on which to draw. In the second, incubation stage, we allow our minds the time and the space to work over these new ideas. From this process, new patterns of thought and fresh ideas form and emerge in the transformation stage.

During the transformation stage we may become conscious of a new direction developing in our lives. We may start to see our relationships and commitments in a new light. Often this can be the start of a major self-initiated personal transition. When this insight occurs we have reached a critical point. We are ready to grasp a new way of thinking and acting. We are ready for action.

Action

Awareness of new possibilities brings us to the fourth stage toward achieving creative change: putting our new ideas into *action*. This may involve activities such as actively seeking a new partner, job or creative business idea, or we might take an overseas job or start a new personal project.

This final stage may also involve letting go of some of our old habits and taking hold of new ones. It requires commitment and motivation to move out of our "comfort zone". We can think of a comfort zone as the bottom of a valley; from there all directions lead upwards. To move out of this comfort zone, we must first set a direction and then develop some *forward momentum*.

Momentum is tremendously important. Our experience with many major projects – and creative personal change is certainly a major project – is that they often fail due to a lack of momentum. Without momentum, new problems are found, people become distracted, energy is dissipated rather than concentrated, and enthusiasm is lost.

But how do you create and then maintain momentum? You do it by continuing to move forward even when you are feeling lazy and don't "feel" like it, by making sustained progress, and by maintaining your long-term focus. The same principle of momentum applied to the NASA space missions during the 1960s and 1970s. When the manned landing on the moon was a clear goal, the project moved forward. Funding was maintained and people were committed and enthusiastic. However, once the moon landing had occurred, the NASA missions lost their clear central goal. The momentum was lost, things stopped happening and eventually the space program's funding was cut.

During the implementation or action stage in the creative process your mood changes completely; discouragement and fear turn to optimism and hope – smiles and energy reappear. You feel centered and focused. Often at this stage people experience a return of purpose and meaning into their lives.

All the methods in this book are designed to help you through this process. They provide the ingredients for achieving lasting and on-going personal change. All you need do is provide the time – and the commitment.

CHAPTER SIXTEEN

PRACTICAL SUGGESTIONS
FOR MAKING
IT HAPPEN

T HE *WAY* we embark on achieving personal success with soul will have an impact on how "successful" we are at making it happen. In this chapter we present just a few thoughts on helpful techniques for making it happen. They are by no means the only ones, and some may work for you while others do not. The key is that each of us has to find what is effective for us.

Great events do not necessarily have great causes.

A. J. P. Taylor

THE MAGIC OF WRITING IT DOWN

Robert Cialdini in his book *Influence: How and Why People Agree to Things* recounts a story about the enormously successful Amway Corporation. Amway asks its salespeople to come up with a goal and then write it down. People commit to these individual sales goals by recording them on paper. This is an extremely effective technique. Amway knows that "there is something magical about writing things down".

Other business organizations also know and use this effectively. Some of them have their customers fill in their sales agreements rather than their salespeople.

Another common way businesses cash in on the "magic" of written declarations is through a tried and true promotional device: the 20-, 50- or 100-word or less testimonial contest, where you can win a big prize by composing a short personal statement that begins with the words "Why I like ...". The statement then goes on to laud the features of whatever the product – say, a cake mix or cleaning product – happens to be.

Companies are willing to incur substantial costs to run these types of contests. The aim is to get as many people as possible to go on record as liking the product. People find praiseworthy features of the product and describe them in short essays. Most importantly, in testifying to the product's appeal, the contestants feel that "magical" pull. They begin to believe what they have written.

We can use this technique in our personal lives. When you come up with ideas or plans, write them down. We should add that, from personal experience, to write them down and then file them or hide them away defeats the purpose. After our first family retreat, we brought home our plan and put it with the rest of the piles of paper that lived in our spare room. We didn't see it again for a while and then became angry with ourselves that we hadn't followed our plan. So, when you have written it down, know where it is and revisit it regularly. Stay focused on the plans you have worked so hard to put together.

> Write down your plans and keep them in front of you. It's like marketing to yourself.

POSITIVE AND NEGATIVE ENERGY

Mario has a middle-management job with a large finance company. He works long hours, longer than many of his colleagues. Mario's office is a great place to go if you feel a bit down on the boss. You can always count on him to provide plenty of negative comments to reinforce your own opinion about the boss or the company. Mention anything about the office – the boss, the amount of work, the coffee, the carpet – anything! If you want to complain, he's your man.

Mario's great at providing negative energy. After twenty minutes or so, you walk out the door of his office feeling fully vindicated. Not only have your complaints been whole-heartedly endorsed, you probably have a whole lot of new ones to think about.

On the other hand, you can talk to Mario about something else. You can talk to him about his passion – Italian culture. Wow – what a difference! Suddenly his face lights up. Some years ago he was the director of a local ethnic festival. He will talk about recent cultural events he has been to and the latest Italian restaurant he's sampled. As he speaks, energy just radiates from him. It's hard to believe it's the same person.

Mario is quite successful in his job, but his soul clearly lies elsewhere. The negative energy he gives off when he talks about his work is a symptom of this.

Almost everything we do has either a positive or a negative influence on us. Positive things make us feel better and more able to cope. These can include people we see, sports we play or music we listen to. These things seem to provide us with *positive energy*.

It is easy to tell who or what generates positive energy for us. We look forward to seeing that person or to doing that thing. We feel better during it and afterwards. Our self-esteem is higher and our outlook more positive. It feels right.

On the other hand, some people we see or activities we do make us feel depressed, bored or angry. They may conflict with our personal values or beliefs. They lower our self-esteem. We feel lethargic while we're with them and afterwards. They seem to reduce our energy and we feel negative.

What provides you with positive and negative energy? If you like, write down the people, activities and situations that generate positive energy for you. Next to this, write down those people, activities and situations that generate negative energy.

Let's look at the negative energy side. You may have no choice about some of the things on this side. They may be part of the job you do, your immediate circle of people, or, for a whole range of other possible reasons, they are simply outside your control. Identify these items among those you have written down. These are the things you cannot change – the ones you may have to live with. What you may have to change is how you respond to them.

Now look at the remaining items on your negative energy side. What could you do about these? The first thing you could do is, like the others, change the way you respond to them, see them in a different way. Try to come up with a positive way to look at them. Alternatively, you may be able to reduce your contact with them (or their impact on you) or eliminate them from your life altogether.

Sometimes we feel that eliminating or reducing our contact with things that have a negative impact on us is "running away". We are constantly told we have to "face up to it", "deal with it" or "learn from it". The argument goes that by doing this, you may continue to feel dissatisfied and challenged by them but eventually you can overcome them. However, there is also the old saying that "you shouldn't just keep hitting your head against a brick wall". And, sometimes we end up "turning the other cheek" so many times that we start to wonder how many cheeks we have!

It is also worth keeping in mind the concept of *opportunity cost* – all that time you spend in contact with things that give you negative energy you could spend doing those things that give you positive energy. Think about it *that* way. Making more time for those things that provide you with positive energy seems to make much more sense in this context.

Now, let's look at the positive energy items. Can you substitute the time you spend on some of those negative energy items with time on these? Think about *why* you don't devote more time to these things.

Increasing your overall positive energy and reducing your involvement in things that make you feel negative are important strategies for achieving personal success. They can reduce your stress level and add more soul to your life. And the things that provide you with positive energy probably represent the things which have more meaning to you.

Finally, think about where you would put money on this list. Does money provide you with positive or negative energy? Most people who do this activity don't put it on either list. But many of us spend quite a lot of time focusing on money. If it doesn't give us positive energy, then it might be better to focus some of this time on some of the other things that do.

DRAWING ON THE PEOPLE AROUND YOU

Change has become very much a part of everyday life. At home, at work and school and in our broader communities, change is ongoing and constant. Alvin Toffler's idea of "future shock" seems all too real for many of us today. One psychologist friend of ours phrased it appropriately when he said, "We're all in transition."

There are many ways in which we cope with change. Research indicates that one of the most effective ways to cope with the stresses of life, in particular with life's transitions, is social support. Social support is the support we seek and gain from the people around us. It can be more cognitive (information that is helpful to us) or it can be emotional. Someone is *there* for us.

It is perhaps not surprising that social support is so effective, since it is really about the relationships we have with other people, something we have spent a great deal of time talking about in this book.

Where mutual support exists, both our own success and the success of others benefit. Furthermore, psychologists tell us that social support is essential for mental health and psychological growth.

Think about the people in *your* support network. One useful way is to draw a map of your social network. Use a circle to represent each individual or group in your network.

Use arrows to show the relationships among people in your network.

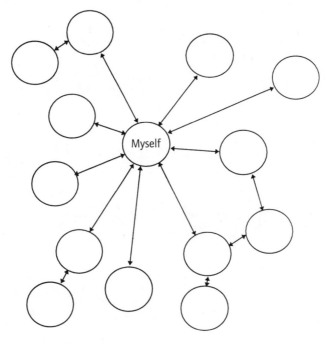

Now assess your network.
- What are the various types of support you need?
- Do the people in your network provide you with what you need?
- Do they help you through change?
- How can you improve your support network?
- What mutual support is there?

This chapter has attempted to give a brief overview of some techniques for putting into action the ideas in this book. It is by no means comprehensive and many other techniques may work for you.

Now, in the final two chapters, we turn from *knowing* and *doing* to *being*...

BEING

CHAPTER SEVENTEEN

REDISCOVERING SOUL

REDISCOVERING SOUL is about finding and nurturing something that exists within each of us. As Tian Dayton, author of *The Quiet Voice of Soul* says, "There is no moment in life when we are separate from soul, no place to go that is without the presence of soul."

We long to journey
without steam or sail!
Help us forget the prison
of our days
and on the canvas of our
minds unfurl
your visions framed by
horizon's gold.

Charles Baudelaire

Rediscovering soul is about engaging in thoughts and activities that are meaningful to us or add meaning to our life. These soul activities create a sense of wholeness and humanness, providing a depth to our lives that inspires and liberates us. Through them we can express our individuality and uniqueness. They help us to become more centered and at peace with ourselves.

No formulas exist for rediscovering soul. What works for one person will not necessarily work for someone else. Because every person is unique, our overall practice for rediscovering soul will also be unique – whatever it is, it should speak directly to us.

One thing is the same for all of us. Soul is not an object to be found, like a lost set of keys. Rediscovering soul is an integral, on-going dynamic in our journey through life.

Nor is soul rediscovery an academic pursuit. Belief in soul is the first step, but *rediscovering soul requires action*. Faith and action combine to make a person a practicing Christian or Jew or Hindu. Similarly with soul, it is faith in soul together with the practice of on-going soul activities which create a life filled with soul.

In this chapter we have included many ideas for creating and enhancing your personal process of soul rediscovery. While a broad range of alternatives are presented, the essence of soul rediscovery is *creative experimentation* – trying different things and seeing what works for you.

Soul can be rediscovered in both the ordinary and the extra-ordinary, in both day-to-day events and once-in-a-lifetime experiences. Soul can be found in newness and excitement, but it can also be found in continuity and similarity.

Walking down the street, shuffling through the fallen leaves, can be a soul experience. Even though this season happens every year – the trees look the same, the leaves look the same – there can be something very special about this experience. Somehow the intense beauty of the season affects us in a way that is hard to describe.

In contrast, the most extraordinary experiences can provide soul. We traveled to the small, mountainous country of Nepal some ten years ago. We spent the first night at a small inn on the foothills of the Himalayas. Early the next morning, we woke up and looked out the small, frosty window of our room. Across the valley, the bright orange glow of the sun was rising over Mount Everest and the other jagged peaks of the Himalayas. It was a sight that sent shivers up our spines. We were struck in this moment by the enormous globe we all walk upon and by contrast our own smallness.

In physics, scientists have discovered *fractal patterns*, identical patterns that exist at many different levels, from the very micro-atomic level right up to the macro, like the shape of a country's shoreline. Soul, too can be found at both the very tiny level – a butterfly floating from flower to flower –

and at the extraordinary, grand level – the weight of tons of water sliding over the falls at Niagara.

Another characteristic of soul is that it is nurtured and strengthened through connection. Connection is what occurs when we experience and develop an understanding of the cultural, social and historical context in which we live – our personal rituals and beliefs or those of our cultural group (events for some like Christmas or Hanukkah), or our social, family or local history. These activities *connect* us with our past and help us understand the present.

Why do these types of connections provide soul? We believe it is because soul thrives on layers of connections and meanings, connections which create richness and complexity. Importantly, these connections help us gain a better understanding of who we are and how each of us is special and unique. Paradoxically, we also gain a better understanding of what we share with others – what makes us the same. In this way, connections create *an internal dialogue within the individual, and an external dialogue with our surroundings.* And where these connections support personal reflection and create depth, there is soul.

Electronic connections, such as television, radio and personal computers, also provide avenues for rediscovering soul. For example, we can learn about our cultural group and strengthen our connection with it through multicultural radio and television. However, this electronic connection can also be soul-destroying, presenting a very narrow view of culture and reality, showing us stereotypes and actively reducing our individuality.

Sometimes connections can be made through coincidence. For example, have you had the experience of chatting to someone – it might be someone you know well or someone you have just met – when suddenly you both realize that you have a mutual acquaintance? How do you feel – excited, "energized", glad and exuberant? Why do you feel like this? Why should finding out you have a mutual friend make you feel good? Once again, it is the excitement of sharing a connection or creating a new one – soul is experienced.

Relationships with our family, partner, friends, work colleagues and other people provide excellent opportunities for rediscovering soul. Through giving, kindness, understanding and care, we can all build deep, loving relationships – relationships filled with soul.

This raises an important point. Soul discovery should not be seen as selfish or self-centered. Like the relationship model of success, it challenges us to improve the quality of our relationships with others.

Soul and emotion are also closely connected. *Activities with a high emotional content are often opportunities for soul rediscovery.*

> Looking at the quality of your relationships will tell you about the condition of your soul.

When Sam's father was dying, Sam spent a great deal of time with him. They had been apart for a long time and Sam saw this as his last real opportunity to reconcile and resolve some of the difficulties in their relationship.

Sam's father Tony had been a famous criminal lawyer and was a man with a strong personality. As Sam reached adulthood, he and his father came head to head in many heated arguments. Whenever Sam tried to exert his manhood, his father would cut him down. Sam would respond by becoming very angry and aggressive. The relationship deteriorated and ended with Sam leaving home and moving interstate.

Sam and his father didn't see each other for many years. Sam established himself in his chosen area of work and went along with his own life. On rare occasions during work-related trips that took him that way, he visited his parents, but the relationship with his father was still strained. Neither would make any effort to resolve their differences.

Sam worked as a contract electrical technician for major telecommunications companies. During the breaks between contracts he renovated his house and studied part-time. One day at home he received a phone call from his mother: Tony was sick – very sick. He was in hospital and the preliminary tests indicated cancer.

Sam was filled with mixed emotions. He still felt deep anger with his father, but he also felt sadness and guilt. How could this have happened? Was he in some way partly to blame? What should he do? Although unsure of what he might do, he decided to start by taking leave from work and going to stay with his parents for some time. He felt he could, at the very least, comfort his mother.

His first visit to see his father was a turning point in their relationship. Tony looked strangely out of place in the hospital. For the first time, Sam noticed the lines of old age etched on Tony's face. He could also see the pain in his father's eyes. By the end of this first visit, Sam knew what he should do; he would help take care of his father.

From Tony's point of view, being faced with his own mortality and weakness was a major shock. He had always been in control of everything. Now his illness had left him barely able to walk. And here was his son, who he had fought with so violently so many times, helping him. It had a profound effect on him.

Over the weeks, Tony and Sam talked about their lives and relationship. They shared more about themselves than they had ever felt comfortable sharing in the past. Sam talked about his house, his job and his friends. He also described his plans to set up his own electrical business. Sometimes, when Tony was too sick to talk, he would just listen and nod to Sam. At other times he would sleep and Sam would read quietly.

After several weeks, it became clear that Tony was not responding to the medical treatment. Through his last few weeks, Sam stayed by his side day and night.

Sam came away from the experience a changed man. With the death of his father, he saw his own life in a new way. He had seen how a proud man could be humbled and this changed how he saw himself and those around him. He resolved to see his mother more often and to reassess his own plans. Rather than setting up his business where he was living, he decided to move closer to his mother.

As we can see from Sam's experience, suffering provides a chance to rediscover soul. Buddhist teachings recognize that suffering is an unavoidable part of life, and that it is how we *respond* to suffering that is important. *Responding to pain, loss and trauma with dignity, courage and forgiveness is a deep experience of soul rediscovery.*

While we have spent some time looking at soul rediscovery through our experiences of the world and our relationships with others, soul can also be found in the quiet times we have by ourselves. Soul is often lost among all the frenetic activity of everyday life. It is easy to "lose the plot" in the rush to get things done. Through activities like meditation or just sitting alone quietly we can be in the "now", live in the moment and reconnect with soul. Meditation quietens, focuses and centers us. It can heal and renew the body, providing spiritual food and reducing stress.

Personal reflection also opens channels to the soul. It can help to build personal integrity, honesty, personal trust and openness. It can challenge us to exercise our conscience and to be true to our personal values. Finally, meditation and personal reflection allow us to listen to our inner voice, to clarify our thinking and to find answers to our concerns.

For some people, religious and spiritual practice are the ways they rediscover soul. Belief, prayer and ritual are soul activities through which people can begin to see the sacredness and wonder in everyday life. Spirituality and religion can provide people with meaning, and they can assist in developing their life's purpose.

Spirituality and religion are not synonymous. Religion involves an institutional structure, religious principles and a set of defined rituals. Spirituality can be our purely personal experience of life or the spiritual journey of "coming to one's own self" or "finding God within ourselves".

In summary, soul can be rediscovered in many ways, through individual activities, such as meditation, or through public activities, such as caring for others. The remainder of this chapter covers more specific activities that may help you rediscover soul. These activities represent only a sample of the infinite possibilities. In thinking about rediscovering soul, a good place to start is to think about those activities which have provided soul for you in the past.

CREATIVITY

We can rediscover soul through creativity. When we do something creative we express our individuality. This process can be a path to personal discovery, enriching our connection with our own self, or it can strengthen the connections we have with others – our self-expression provides ourselves and others with deeper insights into our nature.

Unfortunately, we often feel we do not have the talent or skills to be creative. We often hear people say, "I'm not very creative." But this isn't true. Everyone is creative. It does not require you to be an expert. There are no correct answers.

Creative work can be purely personal. There is no need to show it to anyone else. It doesn't require external recognition. It can simply be about the relationship we have with ourselves.

Leisure activities can be creative and provide us with soul. Gardening, woodworking, needlework, home decorating, cooking, drawing, photography and thousands of other activities allow us to express ourselves. Many people report feeling at peace or intensely "in the moment" when pursuing their favorite leisure activities. Those who enjoy gardening often describe a feeling of being "at one with nature" when they are in the garden. These are all ways of articulating soul experiences or soul moments.

JOURNALS

Soul can be discovered through keeping a diary or journal. A personal diary is a tool for self-reflection that captures events, feelings and insights. Journal writing is creative and personal. It provides connection with the past and greater connection with ourselves.

Doris has kept a journal on and off since about the age of ten. She has a range of cardboard boxes which contain a collection of different colored and shaped journals. Some of them describe the happenings of an entire year. Others are patchy – just thoughts as they came to mind. In some cases, there are strings of years well documented, while other years go virtually undocumented. Tickets, photographs and other mementos of major events are kept as "markers" of what has been her life.

It is incomplete, but that doesn't really matter. *What is more important is the process, not the end-product.* Other journal writers often say the same thing. Few spend much time going back over their old journals. It is the process of writing that is important. It helps make sense of life – integrating all of the amazing and not-so-amazing events that happen – and contributes to the process of personal growth and development. It is a time to "catch up with soul", a time for contemplation of life.

LETTER WRITING

Writing letters can be reflective and creative. The active exchange of letters with someone can increase the connection in our lives. Letter writing, like all the best soul activities, involves both an internal and an external dialogue.

> Letters mingle souls.
> *John Donne*

Years ago, Doris traveled overseas on her own to Europe. It was, in many ways, a personal journey of discovery. In London, on a rare warm and sunny day, she wandered into Hyde Park to write her journal. Walking down a narrow path, she saw many locals out enjoying the sun. Disappointingly, all the park benches lining the path were already occupied. Sharing a bench was the only option, although journal writing is a rather private activity, and she would have preferred a space to herself.

So, as people often do, she sized up the various bench occupants to determine the best bench to share. Maybe there was someone who would be willing to exchange a few words but would then leave her to her writing.

A man with grey hair, black-rimmed glasses and a walking stick was sitting by himself on a bench a few yards ahead. He looked friendly enough without appearing to be a big talker. Doris asked if she could share his bench and he nodded. After a few minutes the man asked Doris what she was writing.

Soon a conversation was struck up. Peter was an American, a retired university professor now living in a little town in Switzerland. Over the course of the conversation a bond developed between this unlikely pair of travelers. Anyway, Doris ended up visiting him in Switzerland later in her trip and, at that stage, wasn't to know that he would become her greatest writing companion.

Over the past twelve years, they have corresponded frequently, sharing with each other what is happening in their lives. Doris has learned a little of what being a man of some sixty years is like and the feelings of getting older. He has shared good advice about how to cope with her life and times.

Every time Doris writes to him or receives a letter, it is a soul experience. "It is an important part of my life. It isn't just interesting. There is something about it, something hard to describe in words."

ART, POETRY AND LITERATURE

Soul discovery can happen through art – painting, sculpture, literature, drawing, dance, theatre, movies and the many other different forms that art takes. Art can affect us in many ways

– emotionally, intellectually, spiritually. It can provide rich and sometimes unusual connections. For example, exhibitions of Van Gogh's paintings are always popular in New York. Why is this? He is, after all, a painter of rural life in nineteenth-century southern France. A number of reasons have been suggested. Van Gogh's energy, dynamic brushstrokes and sometimes claustrophobic style seem to mirror the frantic New York lifestyle. Conversely, his landscapes and purity of subject appear to speak directly to those trapped within the urban landscape. Somehow Van Gogh's work communicates across the decades to us, contrasting with our contemporary city life. And like all great works of art, it has transcended the period in which it was created, still touching us today.

Poetry and literature can provide soul, sparking our imaginations, tugging at our emotions and touching us deeply. It can transport us to other times and places, helping us to see the joys and suffering of others and to experience the richness of life.

> True art, when it happens to us, challenges the 'I' that we are.
>
> *Jeanette Winterson*

Music

Music with soul speaks to us honestly and directly. It is sacred and sometimes profound. This music is not necessarily religious. Many forms of secular music, such as jazz, opera and classical, have soul.

> Stephen collects '60s rhythm and blues music. Among his collection of old 45s is the music of Aretha Franklin, Marvin Gaye, Otis Redding and many others. "For me this music spans the range of human emotions, from joy and celebration, to sadness and despair. On the best records, the singer and the music speak directly and personally, intimately capturing and communicating the feeling embedded in the lyrics. The music – soul music – is aptly named. It is music filled with soul."

Making music – singing or playing either by yourself or in a group – enhances soul. Best of all, both the creative act of making music and the product, the music itself, provide soul food.

Alison has always enjoyed singing – mainly in the shower or in the car, where no one could hear. But then one day, several years ago, while looking through the newspaper, a gospel singing workshop caught her attention. She had always found that type of music inspiring and uplifting so she decided to go along.

However, she wasn't prepared for what happened. "I went along to the workshop just to have some fun singing songs that I enjoyed, but it turned out to be much more. Singing with a group of twenty other people was a powerful experience. I came home feeling transformed, at peace, and somehow, in a way I couldn't explain, more 'connected' with the whole. It took me out of myself and somehow strengthened my ties with everything around me."

MEDITATION

The practice of meditation, which seems relatively new in Western societies, dates back to at least 5000 BC. Meditation centers the mind and body and holds us in the present. It increases the connection we have with ourselves and ultimately the world, so it is a form of soul discovery.

Many methods of meditation exist and many good books describe them, so only a short overview of the process will be given here.

Three main stages of meditation exist, each deeper than the one before it – relaxation, interiorization and expansion. The first stage is the relaxation of the body and the mind. Controlled stretching and breathing relax the muscles and remove tension from the body. Relaxing

Don't just do something – sit there.

Advertisement for a meditation centre

the mind can be achieved using a variety of methods such as controlled deep breathing or listening to music.

Concentration without mental strain is the essence of the second stage – interiorization. While the first stage relaxes the mind and body, this second stage is about achieving concentration of the mind. However, unlike concentrating on a problem or external object, when we meditate our concentration is focused internally, in our own minds. Methods for interiorization include focusing on the "third eye", "watching the breath" and visualization.

When relaxation and concentration of the mind have been achieved, the meditation experience can move into the last phase – expansion of consciousness. Expansion of consciousness is perhaps the ultimate form of connection. It is about connection between ourselves and what is around us to the point where the distinction between the two disappears. This is described variously in Eastern spirituality as being of "one mind", or as a state of enlightenment.

SOUL IS WHERE YOU LIVE

Where you live and your home environment can provide soul. Your home can be the canvas on which you paint your life.

> We live in an inner-city suburb near the university we both attended many years ago. The area has special significance for us. It is part of who we are. It is not simply "a place to live". Walking out the door and around the neighborhood has meaning for us. And while there may be changes in the neighborhood, as people come and go, we find soul here.
>
> Others who visit the area find the parking terrible, the yards small, the traffic annoying and the many students noisy. This is not where they want to live. The area has no soul for them. They would rather live in their newly built houses with their big gardens out among the native trees in the suburbs. That – the quiet bushland surroundings with birds and space – has meaning for them.

SOUL IN PLACES YOU TRAVEL TO

Pilgrimages to places of personal, historical or religious significance provide soul. These places may have personal importance, such as your place of birth, or they may be places which are significant in forming your sense of self. They may also be places you have a spiritual connection with or which have significance in your personal or family history.

Several years after our first trip to India, we returned again. On our first trip we had worked, providing support to a rural health care project. This second trip was a holiday and it included a second visit to the northern Indian city of Varanasi.

Varanasi hugs a long curve of the holy Ganges River. For Hindus, it is Benares, the holiest city in India. It is crammed with temples and pilgrims. The pilgrims wash themselves on the "ghats" or steps that line the river, while sacred cows wander among the faithful.

The old part of the city, down near the river, is a patchwork of narrow, cobbled lanes. Dating back to the days of the silk road, these lanes are too small for cars. Our favorite hotel is located in this quiet part of the city.

One evening we went up to the roof at dusk. Among the other flat roofs, we could look out over the city. The twilight was a soft purple and red fading across the sky. As the city settled into night, thousands of children were on the roof-tops flying small red and blue paper kites. Silently the kites danced in the warm breeze. It was a scene from the Middle Ages, in this timeless, sacred city. Before this fabulous vista, memory and time fused into a pure expression of soul.

NATURE AND THE ENVIRONMENT

Nature and the natural environment provide infinite opportunities for rediscovering soul. The natural beauty, the infinite variety of form and color and the rhythm of the seasons speak directly to us.

Stephen has worked in many parts of the Australian outback, in the deserts of Western Australia and the Northern Territory. Among some of the oldest rocks in the world, sun, wind and rain have carved a unique landscape rich in earthy colors. Timeless and ancient – this is the land of the Aboriginal Dreaming.

Stephen explains, "When I am out there by myself, I find the outback compelling. It is a special and moving place."

SOUL AND OUR RELATIONSHIPS

When we redefined success to integrate soul, we said that success was found in achieving quality relationships. These relationships include our relationships with other people, including partners, children, family and friends.

Relationships with soul are built on honest, open communication, trust and mutual support. They can provide space when it is needed and room for individuals to grow. At the deepest level, our most intimate soul relationships allow us to share our most human characteristics; our deep personal fears as well as our joys, hopes and dreams. *Put quite simply, relationships with soul are relationships with love.*

Unfortunately, when we define success solely in terms of personal fulfillment or competition, soul suffers. Instead of building trust, we create suspicion; rather than open communication, we create defensiveness; instead of mutual support, we generate destructiveness and envy. In these situations, our relationships can often become empty and meaningless, sometimes spiraling into decay.

> To be able to express our most intimate feelings and thoughts without fear of betrayal is one of the great quests of the life of the soul.
>
> *Thomas Moore*

For these reasons, the act of giving to others plays an important role in rediscovering soul.

265

Roslyn's childhood was not a happy one. Her parents' marriage had broken up when she was ten. She had spent most of her teenage years growing up with her grandparents. They had done the best they could, but they could not totally substitute for her parents. Roslyn also felt that her father was to blame for the divorce. He was easy to dislike, being rather cold and distant.

In her early twenties, Roslyn's relationships with other men were not very successful – a string of relationships went nowhere. Many of her partners reminded her of her father. Eventually she resigned herself to the single life.

At college she studied social work, and after graduating, worked for an independent welfare agency for homeless people. Her work involved counseling and care for destitute men and women. The work was challenging and difficult and she generally came home physically and emotionally drained.

However, her counseling provided an insight into the lives of others. Seeing the day-to-day difficulties of others helped her put her own problems into perspective. After several years, Roslyn's relationships with men began to improve. She began to view some of the characteristics of her father more sympathetically as she began to understand them.

When she began dating John, she saw him simply as a friend and work colleague. But slowly their relationship developed into something more. She loved to hear him talk about the people he had worked with and to see the care in his eyes and his hands.

As Roslyn's relationship with John blossomed, she found she could discuss the difficulties of her childhood with him. Through this discussion she was able to resolve some of her long-standing personal problems. When we met her several years later, she was positive, confident and happier than we'd ever seen her.

As Roslyn's experience illustrates, many people who do caring work often say they get more out of it than they put in. Why is this? We believe it is because when we give, we receive soul in return.

Giving and caring is not simply about giving money. Donating money is insufficient to rediscover soul. Money does not connect us with others and it provides little emotional feedback. To rediscover soul, we must give *our time and energy*.

Giving time and energy provides direct and personal feedback. Young people with anorexia provide a very illustrative case of this. The *destruction* in these cases is obvious; these individuals have been preoccupied with self and self-image. One of the most powerful strategies for helping people to overcome anorexia has been encouraging them to become involved in contributing to and helping others.

> When you feel depressed – do something for someone else. The positive feedback you receive will become positive energy to move you forward.

The positive energy of doing things for others is actually physically *healing*. It helps us look beyond ourselves and diverts us from self-centered preoccupations that can be self-destructive. Through contributions to others it becomes possible to develop a deeper understanding of ourselves and other people; and, as in Roslyn's case, life becomes richer.

STORYTELLING

Finally, storytelling is a powerful method for rediscovering soul. Australian Aboriginal people, for example, use storytelling to maintain their cultural traditions, to pass on learning and to connect themselves to the land on which they live.

> Doris's parents grew up in northern Italy during World War II. They lived in a small village in a valley near the Swiss border. Often they will tell stories about their time growing up. The stories are about village life, the war and their relatives and friends. Sometimes the stories are about incidents that occurred, or about the local customs, the local languages and foods. Around the dinner table, that place and time live again and it creates a sense of connection for all of us.

In this chapter we have explored the *being* dimension of life – finding our sense of place and connection to the world. As you can see, soul can look like many different things. We invite you to explore soul in all it forms and in all aspects of your life.

CHAPTER EIGHTEEN

WHERE TO FROM HERE?

Man, unlike any other thing organic or inorganic in the universe, grows beyond his work, walks up the stairs of his concepts, emerges ahead of his accomplishments.

John Steinbeck

THANK YOU for taking this journey with us. We hope you have found it stimulating. It has also been a journey for us, a synthesis of many ideas which have hopefully crystallized onto these pages.

RELATIONSHIPS, SUCCESS AND SOUL

In many ways, we feel that at the heart of this book is a very simple concept: that we can integrate personal success and soul by improving the quality of our relationships. However, like most simple ideas, the test is in the doing – this is where the challenge lies.

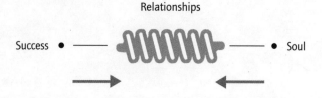

To have authentic relationships we need to express ourselves as we really are. Unfortunately we often place constraints on our individuality, limiting our options of behavior to a narrower and narrower set of socially acceptable norms. Consequently it can then become more difficult to have authentic relationships, so we end up feeling more and more disconnected.

Many of us need to allow more time to build authentic relationships with other people. Otherwise, our network of "real" relationships can diminish, and, along with it, we are diminished. We need to be interconnected – this is where soul lies, in our connections with

> The degree to which we are able to form relationships with others is a measure of the growth we have achieved within ourselves.
>
> *Lewis Brown Griggs*

other people, plants, animals, God and the universe. The richer and deeper this connectivity, the greater the soul in our lives.

This is true of our work settings, our families; all facets of our lives. If we are in competition with our work colleagues, or with members of our family, how can we experience a true relationship? Relationships are founded initially by focusing on similarities – the attributes we all share. Focusing on relationships then allows us to go further and to celebrate the differences and the diversity of life.

Part of what this book is about is redefining your life. This redefining process takes personal courage and includes some risks. You will need to stand up to those who do not like the way you have chosen to redefine your life, but it is worth it for the satisfaction of turning your life into one in which you do what is important to you. And for the soul that becomes an everyday part of it when you stamp your impression on every part of your life.

As you embark on this journey you will also find that you not only unleash more of your own personal potential, you will also unleash other people's potential. That is one of the most exciting aspects of operating out of the relationship model of success – it affects everything and everyone around you. Like when a stone is dropped into a pond, the waves radiate out in all directions.

Why is the relationship model of success so necessary today?

The increasing connection we have to the world through the communications revolution presents us with a profound challenge and a unique opportunity – to develop a set of global values. We are already beginning to see these global values developing with the increasing acceptance of free market principles, the universal condemnation of terrorism and the rise of the partnership model of leadership.

However, we are also seeing values such as true individuality being threatened and an increasing tolerance for violence, selfishness and poverty as part of the status quo. This is clearly not part of the relationship model of success. As we have already discussed, *knowing* is not enough; *doing* is necessary.

We all have a role to play in ensuring that those universal values are ones we would like to see our children inherit. What will those values be? Future generations will surely evaluate our success or failure based on the legacy we leave them.

Many of the concerns facing businesses and organizations are similar to those faced by individuals. Environmental considerations, managing scarce resources and better decision-making are all issues for people within and outside companies. And while the overall purpose, objectives and goals may be different, both groups have a vested interest in developing effective new tools and insights. We can no longer separate personal development from organizational development.

There are now significant opportunities to draw on experience and expertise from a wider range of disciplines and fields of endeavor. This cross-pollination is only likely to increase as more individuals change professions.

In the near future, we may see increased application of business sciences such as organizational theory to social systems, while companies may look increasingly towards the fields of science and psychology for methods to facilitate organizational change.

In addition, as business organizations are becoming the dominant institutions in our society, a new range of challenges presents itself. Organizations will have to find new ways to care for the souls of their employees as well as providing opportunities for personal success. Success with soul is not just a personal issue; it is an issue for all our social institutions.

Finally, by acting out of the relationship model of success we will begin to address many of the emotional, spiritual, social, organizational and environmental problems that remain unaddressed. Slowly our sense of disillusionment, emptiness and loss of meaning will be diminished. We will be able to focus energy positively and successfully, where it benefits ourselves, others and the world around us.

Then we will truly be able to achieve success with soul.

Bibliography

Ameriks, K. (1982). *Kant's Theory of Mind.* Oxford, UK: Clarendon Press.

Barron, F. (1969). *Creative Person and Creative Process.* Florida: Holt, Rinehart & Winston.

Baudelaire, C. (1982). *The Flowers of Evil.* Boston, MA: David R. Godine.

Beach, B. (1989). *Integrating Work and Family Life: The Home-Working Family.* Albany: State University of New York Press.

Boostrom, R. (1992). *Developing Creative & Critical Thinking.* Lincolnwood, IL: NTC Publishing Group.

Boyd, Rev. J. H. (1994). *Affirming the Soul.* Cheshire, CT: Soul Research Institute.

Brammer, L. M. (1991). *How to Cope with Life Transitions: The Challenge of Personal Change.* New York: Hemisphere Publishing Corporation.

Bremmer, J. (1983). *The Early Greek Concept of Soul.* New Jersey: Princeton University Press.

Britton, K. (1969). *Philosophy and the Meaning of Life.* London: Cambridge University Press.

Burger, J. M. (1985). Desire for control and achievement-related behaviors. *Journal of Personality and Social Psychology,* 48(6), 1520–1533.

Burger, J. M. (1992). *Desire for Control: Personality, Social and Clinical Perspectives.* New York: Plenum Press.

Burhoe, R. W. (1973). "Civilisation of the Future". *Philosophy Forum,* 13, 171–173.

Caes, C. J. (1985). *Beyond Time.* Lanham, MD: University Press of America.

Canfield, J. & Hansen, M. V. (1993). *Chicken Soup for the Soul.* Deerfield Beach, Florida: Health Communications.

Canfield, J. (1995). Rekindling the fires of your soul. In R. Carlson & B. Shield (Eds), *Handbook for the Soul,* pp. 87–94. Sydney, Australia: Doubleday.

Capra, F. (1985). *The Tao of Physics.* London: Fontana Press.

Carlson, R. & Shield, B. (Eds) (1995). *Handbook for the Soul.* Sydney, Australia: Doubleday.

Chappell, T. (1993). *The Soul of a Business.* New York: Bantam Books.

Cialdini, R. B. (1984). *Influence: How and Why People Agree to Things.* New York: Quill William Morrow.

Cohen, J.M. & Cohen, M.J. (1995). *Dictionary of Twentieth-Century Quotations.* London: Penguin.

Cotton, R. (1996). *Reinventing Success.* Sydney: Random House.

Cousineau, P. (1995). *Soul: An Archaeology.* London: Thorsons.

Covey, S. (1989). *The Seven Habits of Highly Effective People.* New York: Simon & Schuster.

Cushman, D. P. & McPhee, R. D. (1980). *Message–Attitude–Behavior Relationship.* New York: Academic Press.

Dayton, T. (1995). *The Quiet Voice of the Soul.* Deerfield Beach, Florida: Health Communications.

DeVries, W. A. (1988). *Hegel's Theory of Mental Activity.* Ithaca, NY: Cornell University Press.

Dominguez, J. & Robin, V. (1992). *Your Money or Your Life.* New York: Viking.

Drucker, P. F. (1992). *Managing for the Future.* New York: Truman Talley/ Plume.

Drucker, P. F. (1995). *Post-Capitalist Society.* New York: HarperCollins.

Eitner, L. (1970). *Neoclassicism and Romanticism 1750–1850.* Sources & Documents in the History of Art Series, Vol. 2, *Restoration/Twilight of Humanism.* H. W. Janson (Ed.). Englewood Cliffs, NJ: Prentice-Hall.

Etzioni, A. (1995). Normative-affective factors: Towards a new decision-making model. In M. Zey (Ed.). *Decision Making: Alternatives to Rational Choice Models.* Newbury Park, CA: Sage.

Fisher, S. & Cooper, C. L. (Eds) (1990). *On the Move: The Psychology of Change and Transition.* West Sussex, UK: Wiley.

Flew, A. (Ed.)(1964). *Body, Mind, and Death.* Problems of Philosophy Series, P. Edwards (Ed.). New York: Macmillan.

Frank, S. L. (1993). *Man's Soul: An Introductory Essay in Philosophical Psychology.* (B. Jakim, Trans.). Athens: Ohio University Press.

Frankl, V. E. (1984). *Man's Search for Meaning.* New York: Washington Square Press.

Gauld, A. & Shotter, J. (1977). *Human Action and its Psychological Investigation.* London: Routledge & Kegan Paul.

Gawain, S. (1978). *Creative Visualisation.* New York: Bantam Books.

Gibran, K. (1926). *The Prophet.* London: William Heinemann.

Gleick, J. (1987). *Chaos: Making a New Science.* New York: Viking.

Greene, M. (1972). *Hegel on the Soul.* The Hague, Netherlands: Martinus Nijhoff.

Griggs, L. B. & Louw, L. L. (Eds) (1995). *Valuing Diversity: New Tools for a New Reality.* New York: McGraw-Hill.

Hayes, J. R. (1989). *The Complete Problem Solver*. Hillside, NJ: Erlbaum.

Hickman, C. R. (1990). *Mind of a Manager, Soul of a Leader*. New York: Wiley.

Jackson, M.R. (1984). *Self-Esteem and Meaning: A Life Historical Investigation*. New York: State University of New York Press.

Jagdish Chander, Raj Yogi B. K. (1980). *Human Values, Moral Values and Spiritual Values*. Delhi, India: Prajapita Brahmi Kumaris.

Janis, I. L. & Mann, L. (1977). *Decision Making: A Psychological Analysis of Conflict, Choice and Commitment*. New York: The Free Press.

Janson, H. W. (1971). *A Basic History of Art*. Englewood Cliffs, NJ: Prentice-Hall.

Joyce, J. (1916). *A Portrait of the Artist as a Young Man*. London: Granada.

Jung, C. G. (Ed.) (1978). *Man and His Symbols*. London: Pan Books.

Jung, C. G. (1995). *Memories, Dreams and Reflections* (R. & C. Winston, Trans.). London: Fontana Press.

Katzenbach, J. R. & Smith, D. K. (1993). *The Wisdom of Teams*. Boston, MA: Harvard Business School Press.

Klinger, E. (1977). *Meaning & Void: Inner Experience and the Incentives in People's Lives*. Minneapolis: University of Minnesota Press.

Kofodimos, J. (1993). *Balancing Act: How Managers Can Integrate Successful Careers and Fulfilling Personal lives*. San Francisco: Jossey-Bass.

Lachs, J. & Scott, C. E. (Eds) (1981). *The Human Search: An Introduction to Philosophy*. New York: Oxford University Press.

Laszlo, E. & Wilbur, J. B. (1971). *Human Values and the Mind of Man*. New York: Gordon & Breach.

Lewis, D. (1992). *Stress for Success*. New York: Carroll & Graf.

Lorenz, K. (1983). *The Waning of Humaneness*. London: Unwin Hyman Limited.

Lovelock, J. E. (1987). *Gaia*. New York: Oxford University Press.

McCormick, D. W. (1994). Spirituality and management. *Journal of Managerial Psychology*, 9(6), 5–8.

Macy, J. (1991). *Mutual Causality in Buddism and General Systems Theory*. Albany: State University of New York Press.

Mandela, N. (1994). *Long Walk to Freedom*. London: Little, Brown and Company.

Mandell, A. cited in J. Gleick (1987). *Chaos: Making a New Science*, p. 298. New York: Viking.

Mann, L. (1989). Becoming a better decision maker. *Australian Psychologist*, 24(2), 141–155.

Mill, J. S. (1910). *Utilitarianism, Liberty, and Representative Government*. London: J. M. Dent & Sons.

Moore, T. (1992). *Care of the Soul*. New York: HarperCollins.

Morris, T. (1994). *True Success*. New York: Berkley Books.

Mullen, J. D. & Roth, B. M. (1991). *Decision-Making: Its Logic and Practice*. Lanham, MD: Rowman & Littlefield Publishers.

Nicholson, N. (1990). The transition cycle: Causes, outcomes, processes and forms. In S. Fisher & C. L. Cooper (Eds) *On the Move: The Psychology of Change and Transition*, pp. 83–108. West Sussex, UK: Wiley.

Norden-Powers, C. (1994). *Empowerment*. Melbourne: The Business Library.

Novak, J. (1993). *How to Meditate*. Bombay: Jaico Publishing House.

Oech, R. V. (1983). *A Whack on the Side of the Head*. New York: Warner Books.

Olson, J. M. (1993). Attitudes and attitude change. *Annual Review of Psychology*, 44, 117–54.

Orwell, G. (1949). 1984. New York: Harcourt Brace Jovanovick.

Osborne, R. (1995). Company with a soul. *Industry Week*, 244(9), 21–26.

Page, S. (1994). *Now That I'm Married, Why Isn't Everything Perfect?* Melbourne: Bookman Press.

Partington, A. (Ed.) (1992). *The Oxford Dictionary of Quotations* (4th edn). Oxford, UK: Oxford University Press.

Pearson, C. S. (1991). *Awakening the Heroes Within*. New York: HarperCollins.

Perkins-Reed, M. (1996). *Thriving in Transition*. New York: Touchstone.

Peters, T. (1994). *The Tom Peters Seminar*. New York: Macmillan.

Pirsig, R. M. (1974). *Zen and the Art of Motorcycle Maintenance*. New York: Bantam Books.

Prigogine, I. & Stengers, I. (1984). *Order out of Chaos*. London: Fontana.

Quinlivan-Hall, D. & Renner, P. (1990). *In Search of Solutions*. Canada: Training Associates Ltd.

Rifkin, J. (1995). *The End of Work*. New York: G.P. Putnam's Sons.

Rokeach, M. (1973). *The Nature of Human Values*. New York: The Free Press.

Saddhatissa, H. (1970). *Buddhist Ethics: Essence of Buddhism*. New York: George Braziller.

Saponaro, M. (1950). *Michelango*. New York: Pellegrini & Cudahy.

Sardello, R. (1992). *Facing the World with Soul*. New York: HarperCollins.

Schwartz, S. H. (1992) Universals in the content and structure of values: Theoretical advances and empirical tests in 20 countries. *Advances in Experimental Social Psychology*, 25, pp. 1–65.

Schwartz, S. H. (1994). Are there universal aspects in the structure and contents of human values? *Journal of Social Issues*, 50(4), 19–45.

Schwarzer, R. (Ed.) (1992). *Self-Efficacy: Thought Control of Action*. USA: Hemisphere.

Senge, P. M. (1990). *The Fifth Discipline*. Sydney: Random House.

Shepherd, E. & Watson, J. P. (1982). *Personal Meanings*. Chichester, UK: Wiley.

Sher, B. (1994). *I Could Do Anything If I Only Knew What It Was*. New York: Dell.

Singer, P. (1995). *How Are We to Live?* New York: Prometheus Books.

Sivananda, S. Sri. (1946). *Ethical Teachings*. Uttar Pradesh, India: Forest Academy Press.

Spence, J. T. & Helmreich, R. L. (1983). Achievement-related motives and behaviors. In J. T. Spence (Ed.) *Achievement and Achievement Motives: Psychological and Sociological Approaches*. San Francisco: Freeman.

Spencer, L. J. (1989). *Winning Through Participation*. Dubuque, IA: Kendall/Hunt.

Stephenson Bond, D. (1993). *Living Myth: Personal Meaning as a Way of Life*. Boston, MA: Shambhala.

Strasser, A. (1996). Existential psychotherapy. *Psychotherapy in Australia*, 2(3), 42–45.

Strasser, S. (1957). *The Soul in Metaphysical and Empirical Psychology*. New York: The Ad Press.

Stromberg, G. (1940). *The Soul of the Universe*. USA: David McKay Company.

Subrahmanian, N. S. (1980). *The Bhagawadgita*. India: Vikas Publishing House.

Tarnas, R. (1996). *The Passion of the Western Mind*. London: Pimlico.

Toffler, A. (1970). *Future Shock*. London: Pan Books.

Trefil, J. (1992). *1001 Things Everyone Should Know About Science*. New York: Doubleday.

Weisbord, M. R. (1987). *Productive Workplaces*. San Francisco: Jossey-Bass.

Wheatley, M. J. (1992). *Management and the New Science*. San Francisco: Berrett-Koehler.

Williams, R. B. (1993). *More Than 50 Ways to Build Team Consensus.* Palatine, IL: IRI/Skylight Training and Publishing.
Winterson, J. (1995). Art Objects. *World Art,* 4, 76–83.

Permissions acknowledgments

Lyrics from "Once In A Lifetime" by David Byrne/Brian Eno/Frantz/Weymouth. Copyright © Warner/Chappell Music. Reproduced by permission of Warner/ Chappell Music Australia Pty Ltd. Unauthorised Reproduction is Illegal.
Script excerpt from "Absolutely Fabulous" Copyright © Jennifer Saunders. Reproduced by permission of Jennifer Saunders and Peters Fraser & Dunlop, UK.
Excerpt from "The Fifth Discipline" by Peter M. Senge Copyright © Peter M. Senge. Reproduced by permission of Doubleday Dell Publishing Group, Inc., USA.
Excerpt from "Celebration – A World of Art and Ritual" Copyright © 1982 Smithsonian Institution. Reproduced by permission of Smithsonian Institution Press, USA.
Quote by Kurt Vonnegut excerpt from David Mamet Interview in *The Guardian* Copyright © 1989 *The Guardian*. Reproduced by permission of *The Guardian*, UK.
Excerpt from "Travelers" by Charles Baudelaire from *Les Fleurs du Mal* Translation copyright © 1982 Richard Howard. Reproduced by permission of David R. Godine, Publisher, Inc., USA.
Quote from A. J. P. Taylor excerpt from obituary in *The Independent* Copyright © 1990 *The Independent*. Reproduced by permission of *The Independent*, UK.
Excerpt from "A Servant to Servants" by Robert Frost from *Poetry of Robert Frost* Copyright © Robert Frost. Henry Holt & Co. Copyright © Robert Frost.
Excerpt from "The Black Cottage" by Robert Frost from *Poetry of Robert Frost* Copyright © Robert Frost. Henry Holt & Co. Copyright © Robert Frost.
Quote from Albert Einstein excerpt from *Reader's Digest* Copyright © 1977 Albert Einstein. Reproduced by permission of The Reader's Digest Association, Inc., USA.
Excerpt from "Civilisation of the Future" by Ralph Wendell Burhoe in *The Philosophy Forum* Copyright © 1973 Ralph Wendell Burhoe. Reproduced by permission of Gordon and Breach Publishing Group, Switzerland.
Excerpt from *The Second Penguin Krishnamurti Reader* by J. Krishnamurti Copyright © J. Krishnamurti. Reproduced by permission of Krishnamurti Foundation Trust, UK.
Excerpt from *Valuing Diversity* by Lewis Brown Griggs and L. L. Louw Copyright © 1995 Lewis Brown Griggs and L. L. Louw.
Excerpt from *Empowerment* by Christo Norden-Powers – The Business Library Copyright © 1994 Christo Norden-Powers. Reproduced by permission of Christo Norden-Powers and The Business Library, Australia. Available from the author Christo Norden-Powers, P.O. Box 192, St. Ives, NSW, 2075 Australia, Phone/Fax +61 2 9440 0022.
Excerpt from *Managing for the Future* by Peter F. Drucker Copyright © 1992 Peter F. Drucker.
Excerpt from "The Hollow Men" in *Collected Poems 1909–1962* by T. S. Eliot, Copyright © 1964, 1963, by T. S. Eliot. Reproduced by permission of Faber and Faber Limited, UK and Harcourt Brace & Company, USA.
Excerpt from *Zen and The Art of Motorcycle Maintenance* by Robert M. Pirsig – William Morrow & Company, Inc. Copyright © 1974 Robert M. Pirsig.